THE
JOHN WAYNE
MOVIES TRIVIA BOOK

THE
JOHN WAYNE
MOVIES TRIVIA BOOK

By LEONARD BRIDEAU

BONANZA BOOKS
New York

To my Ilsa

I wish to thank several friends and associates who gave me their support, encouragement, and in some cases, their determination during the writing of this book. So not to offend anyone, I have taken the writer's prerogative and will alphabetize their names. Again, my special thanks to Chris Brideau, John Costello, Bob Dandrea and to Mike O'May.

This 1989 edition is published by Bonanza Books, distributed by
Crown Publishers, Inc., 225 Park Avenue South, New York, New York 10003,
by arrangement with Raymond Enterprises, Inc.

Printed and Bound in the United States of America

The layout of this book was done by Barbara Kimbrough,
with original illustrations by Lubo Talevski.

Library of Congress Cataloging-in-Publication Data

Brideau, Leonard.
The John Wayne movies trivia book / by Leonard Brideau.
p.   cm.
Bibliography: p.
ISBN 0-517-67673-7
1. Wayne, John. 1907—Miscellanea. 2. Motion pictures—United
States—Miscellanea.   I. Title.
PN2287. W454B75   1989
791.43′028′0924—dc19
89-446
CIP

ISBN 0-517-67673-7
h g f e d c b a

"When the legend becomes fact, print the legend."
from The Man Who Shot Liberty Valance

On October 28, 1980, in the Cleveland Conference Center, a young reporter approached the Republican presidential candidate Ronald Reagan following his face to face televised debate with Jimmy Carter and asked him what it felt like being on the same stage with the President of the United States. Mr. Reagan smiled and answered it was nothing since he had been on stage with John Wayne.

TABLE OF CONTENTS

CHAPTER ONE

JOHN WAYNE: THE BASIC TRIVIA

Who is John Wayne? Well, unlike any other movie star before him, John Wayne, The Duke, became an American Institution. The Duke was a legend in his own lifetime and his name has come to symbolize a particular brand of hero...the American Cowboy. To the movie going public he was their personal hero for over fifty years. To his nation and the world at large, he represented America and its national traits of courage, toughness and decency. John Wayne fans always knew their hero would triumph over the obstacles facing him in each of his movies. Audiences identified with The Duke and the characters he played, and he never disappointed them. So, before we begin the chapters on the movie career of John Wayne entitled THE DUKE ON FILM, let's start with a simple list of trivia questions about the man himself. After all, any John Wayne fan has to know about the man behind the legend.

1. John Wayne was born where?

   a. Newport, California
   b. Winterset, Iowa
   c. Cape Elizabeth, Maine
   d. Palmdale, California

2. What year was he born?

   a. February 1, 1895
   b. May 26, 1907
   c. June 15, 1903

3. What is The Duke's real name?

   a. John Ethan Wayne
   b. Marion Michael Morrison
   c. Michael Patrick Wayne

4. John Wayne's father was born in:

   a. Indiana
   b. Illinois
   c. Iowa
   d. California

5. Where was John Wayne's mother born?

   a. Ohio
   b. Indiana
   c. Nebraska
   d. Iowa

6. What was John Wayne's nationality?

   a. Irish
   b. English
   c. Scottish
   d. all of the above

7. John Wayne's father was called "Doc" by his friends. What was his occupation?

   a. Dentist
   b. Physician
   c. Druggist
   d. Veterinarian

8. John Wayne's lifelong nickname was Duke. How did he get this name?

   a. He was named after an Irish Duke.
   b. He was given the name by John Ford.
   c. He was named after a pet Airedale terrier.
   d. He took the name from a screen character.

9. Future superstar John Wayne attended what high school in California?

   a. Hollywood High School
   b. Glendale High School
   c. Los Angeles High School

10. Big John Wayne was more than a movie expression. How tall was The Duke in real life?

    a. 6 feet, two inches
    b. 6 feet, three inches
    c. 6 feet, four inches
    d. 6 feet, seven inches

11. After graduating from high school, The Duke wanted to fulfill his father's dreams and attend what school?

    a. Harvard
    b. West Point Military Academy
    c. Yale
    d. Naval Academy

12. Unable to attend the original college of his choice, The Duke enrolled at what college?

    a. Stanford
    b. USC
    c. UCLA

13. The Duke had a scholarship to attend college in what sport?

    a. Basketball
    b. Baseball
    c. Football

14. What position did The Duke play in his chosen sport?

    a. Basketball center
    b. Football tackle
    c. Baseball pitcher

15. What college fraternity did The Duke belong to?

    a. Sigma Phi
    b. Sigma Chi
    c. Delta Epsilon

16. What was The Duke's major while in college?

    a. he was a pre-med student
    b. he was a pre-law student
    c. he was an engineering major

17. The Duke's athletic career in college ended prematurely. Why?

    a. He suffered a serious ankle injury.
    b. He suffered a serious shoulder injury.
    c. He suffered a serious back injury.
    d. He quit to work in the movies.

18. How long did The Duke attend college?

    a. until he graduated with honors
    b. until his senior year
    c. until his sophomore year

19. During school breaks, what Western movie star helped get summer jobs for Wayne and his school friends?

    a. Buck Jones
    b. Tom Mix
    c. Hoot Gibson

20. The first movie studio that The Duke worked for while still a college student was?

    a. Warner Bros.
    b. Paramount Pictures
    c. Fox Studios
    d. Republic Pictures

21. John Wayne's first job in the movies was as:

    a. an assistant stuntman
    b. a fourth assistant propman
    c. a junior carpenter

22. John Wayne first appeared on the movie screen in what early film?

    a. The Drop Kick
    b. Hangman's House
    c. Mother Machree

23. The first movie that The Duke received screen credit for his brief part was:

    a. Words and Music
    b. Salute
    c. Men Without Women

24. What was the first screen name that The Duke used?

    a. John Wayne
    b. Duke Morrison
    c. Pete Donahue

25. When The Duke was given his first "big break" in movies, he was given his new name. Who gave The Duke his screen name?

    a. John Ford
    b. Howard Hawks
    c. Raoul Walsh

26. Young John Wayne was given the starring role along with his new screen name in the early big budget western entitled:

    a. The Virginian
    b. The Big Trail
    c. The Great Train Robbery

27. The Duke was not the original choice for his first starring role. What contemporary and off-screen friend was the studio's first choice?

    a. Ward Bond
    b. Gary Cooper
    c. Lloyd Nolan
    d. Randolph Scott

28. Finally, speaking of names, The Duke's movie name was reportedly chosen because:

    a. it sounded American and western
    b. it was the name of a war hero
    c. it sounded strong and masculine

29. In his private life, The Duke was considered a true gentleman and a one-woman man. How many times was he married?

   a. One time
   b. Two times
   c. Three times
   d. Four times

30. What did The Duke's wives have in common?

   a. they were all screen actresses
   b. they were all of Hispanic background
   c. they were all singers

31. John Wayne loved his children and was very proud of his family. How many children did The Duke have?

   a. Three
   b. Four
   c. Seven

32. How many grandchildren did the Duke have at the time of his death?

   a. 15
   b. 18
   c. 21

33. John Wayne was very proud to be an American. At the start of World War II, he tried to enlist in the Navy, but was rejected because of:

   a. his age
   b. his four dependents
   c. his old college sports injury
   d. all of the above

34. The Duke's movie career spanned the years from 1928 to 1976. When he died in 1979, how many films had he made during his acting career?

   a. 153
   b. 172
   c. 192
   d. 222

35. Some of The Duke's very early Westerns were actually remakes of a famous silent screen western hero. This western hero was:

   a. Tom Mix
   b. Ken Maynard
   c. Buck Jones

36. During The Duke's fifty year movie career, he was all but one of the following:

   a. producer
   b. screenwriter
   c. director

The Duke as The Ringo Kid in the role that made him a star in the 1939 classic Stagecoach.

The Duke's original birth certificate read Marion Robert Morrison, born May 26, 1907. His middle name was changed four years later when his family gave his middle name to his brother Robert Morrison.

The Duke never legally changed his name to John Wayne. He signed legal documents Marion Morrison and seldom responded to the first name of John, preferring to be called Duke instead.

The Duke appeared in 37 films in which his character had the first name John.

Wayne also apeared in six films in which he was named Duke.

Young Marion Morrison was president of his senior high school class at Glendale High School in California.

John Wayne's first screen credit was in the 1929 FOX movie called Words and Music in which he used his real name Duke Morrison.

When The Duke became John Wayne for his first starring role in the 1931 film The Big Trail, he received the huge sum of $75.00 per week.

During a state visit to America, Japan's Emperor Hirohito was given his choice of meeting three American public figures. The first man he asked to meet was John Wayne.

The Duke was once described as an extra star on the American Flag.

37. John Wayne's popularity at the box office will never be equalled. He was among the top ten box office attractions in the Motion Picture Herald box office poll for how many years?

    a. 15
    b. 23
    c. 24
    d. 25

38. John Wayne was the first major motion picture star to:

    a. be given a percentage of the profits
    b. form his own production company
    c. sign a multi-picture million dollar contract
    d. all of the above

39. The Duke's own movie production company was called Batjac Productions. The name came from an early Wayne movie and was the name of a shipping company. The movie was:

    a. Reap the Wild Wind
    b. Wake of the Red Witch
    c. The Sea Chase

40. The first movie that John Wayne produced was:

    a. Red River
    b. Hondo
    c. Angel and the Badman

41. The first movie that John Wayne directed was:

    a. McQ
    b. The Alamo
    c. Green Berets

42. The Academy Award is the dream of all actors and John Wayne was no exception. How many times was The Duke nominated for the Oscar?

    a. One time
    b. Two times
    c. Three times

43. The Duke was the first major star to publicly announce that he had beaten the big C. He underwent surgery for lung cancer in 1965. What was his first film following major surgery.

    a. The War Wagon
    b. McLintock
    c. The Sons of Katie Elder

44. The Duke finally won the Oscar for what film late in his career?

    a. Sands of Iwo Jima
    b. True Grit
    c. The Shootist

45. As he grew older his health failed and he made fewer motion pictures. The Duke's last film was:

a. Rooster Cogburn
b. Beau John
c. The Shootist

46. The Duke often joked about being called a "living legend." What statement about John Wayne is true?

a. he wore false teeth
b. he had one glass eye
c. he wore a toupee

47. Just before his death in 1979, John Wayne was given an honor befitting a legend. Congress awarded him what special honor?

a. The Legend of Merit
b. A gold medal minted in his honor
c. The Congressional Medal of Honor

A young John Wayne once played a corpse in the 1931 Columbia film The Deceiver.

The Duke's first starring film The Big Trail was such a financial failure that it bankrupted FOX studios and sent its head, William Fox to jail. From the ashes of FOX Studios, 20th Century-Fox was formed.

During his years on Poverty Row, John Wayne once shared top billing with a white horse called DUKE— The Miracle Horse.

The Duke is credited with being the movies first singing cowboy. He appeared as Singin' Sandy Saunders in the 1933 "B" Western Riders of Destiny. For the record, The Duke's singing voice as Singin' Sandy was dubbed by a little known singer named Smith Ballew.

It is interesting to note that the film technique used in the Duke's first starring film The Big Trail was twenty years ahead of its time when released in 1930. In 1950 it would be known as CinemaScope.

When Stagecoach was released on February 15, 1939, it was the Duke's 71st film and the end to his career in B and C westerns.

The Duke always wore his wrist-watch military combat style with the watch turned inside on his wrist.

The Duke was a gentleman both on and off-screen. He refused to do scenes that required him to curse or to hit women.

The Duke as Thomas Dunson from the western classic Red River.

CHAPTER TWO

THE DUKE ON FILM...THE MAJOR CLASSICS

John Wayne left to his fans and film historians a legacy of screen work that includes some of the greatest motion pictures ever made. Starting in 1939 with STAGECOACH and ending in 1976 with THE SHOOTIST, Wayne starred in dozens of westerns and action films that have become genuine cinema classics. The total body of John Wayne's cinematic work is without equal in motion picture history spanning almost fifty years. He developed and perfected a screen character whose presence went beyond the confining limits of the movie screen to become part of America's folklore. John Wayne the movie cowboy and super hero became America's hero and legend, and what he stood for on the screen carried over into real life. Fortunately for future generations, television and VCR technology make it possible to repeatedly enjoy the Duke's greatest screen performances. The following pages contain trivia questions from The Duke's movie career. I have ranked the movies into six groups beginning with the ten best John Wayne films.

Remember, with nearly two hundred films to his credit, it is difficult for a John Wayne fan to pick his ten best movies. Moreover, the true John Wayne fan will watch any John Wayne film that is being shown either on television or at a Wayne film festival at the local theater. However, even the most diehard Wayne fan will admit that there are genuine classics among his films that always come to mind when you discuss his movies with friends. The ten films listed below are generally regarded by film historians as true movie classics and The Duke's best screen work. So let's begin.

RANK	MOVIE TITLE	YEAR MADE
1	The Searchers	1956
2	Red River	1948
3	She Wore a Yellow Ribbon	1949
4	True Grit	1969
5	Stagecoach	1939
6	The Shootist	1976
7	The Quiet Man	1952
8	Rio Grande	1950
9	Sands of Iwo Jima	1949
10	Three Godfathers	1948

NUMBER ONE: THE SEARCHERS

1. The movie audience first sees Ethan Edwards (JOHN WAYNE) slowly riding towards his brother Aaron's ranch house. Where is he coming from?

    a. he has just escaped from the territorial prison
    b. he is returning from the Civil War
    c. he is returning from a long cattle drive

2. In what state does the action in The Searchers take place?

    a. Texas
    b. Kansas
    c. Arkansas

3. Ethan fought in the recent war. What side did he fight on?

   a. The Union side
   b. The Confederate side

4. What rank did Ethan Edwards hold in the military?

   a. He was a Captain.
   b. He was a Colonel.
   c. He was a Sergeant.

5. Where did Aaron think his brother had gone after the war?

   a. Mexico
   b. California
   c. Texas

6. Ethan offers to pay his own way while at his brother's ranch. How much money does he give Aaron?

   a. 60 double eagle gold coins
   b. 120 double eagle gold coins
   c. 180 double eagle gold coins

7. What did Ethan give his niece Debbie as a present?

   a. a small pony
   b. a gold coin
   c. a war medal
   d. a sword

8. How does the movie audience learn that Aaron's wife cares a great deal for Ethan?

   a. The preacher sees them kissing.
   b. The tender and loving way she strokes Ethan's army coat.
   c. She tells her husband during an argument.

9. Why does Ethan leave his brother's ranch with the posse?

   a. The Indians have attacked the stagecoach
   b. The Indians have stolen some cattle
   c. The Indians have left the reservation

10. What tribe of Indians are the searchers after?

    a. Apache
    b. Cheyenne
    c. Cherokee
    d. Comanche

11. What is the name of the rag doll that Debbie took with her when she hid from the Indians?

    a. Raggedy Ann
    b. Topsy
    c. Toto

12. When Ethan and the posse find a dead Indian in a shallow grave what does he do?

    a. scalps the dead Indian
    b. smashes the Indian's head with a stone
    c. shoots the dead Indian's eyes out

13. Ethan (Wayne) returns to camp after searching alone for his nieces. Harry Carey, Jr. and Jeffrey Hunter ask him what happened to his Johnny Reb overcoat. What did he do with the coat?

a. It fell off his horse.
b. He buried his niece Lucy in it.
c. He left it as a trail marker.

14. Before starting the search again, Ethan reads a letter from a trader named Futterman. What did the trader send in his letter?

a. a map with the location of the Indians' camp
b. a piece of Debbie's apron
c. Debbie's small rag doll

15. What is the Indian chief's name who Ethan is after?

a. Geronimo
b. Scar
c. Yellow Knife

16. When Ethan finally meets the chief face-to-face, what does the Indian call him?

a. He Who Follows
b. Big Shoulders
c. Quiet One

17. Once inside the tent, the Chief taunts Ethan by showing him his collection of scalps and

a. the skulls of his enemies.
b. Ethan's Confederate war medal around his neck.
c. Ethan's sister-in-law's scalp on a lance.

18. Ethan's hatred for the Comanche is dramatized when he attempts to kill Debbie, now a squaw. He is stopped from shooting her when

a. Martin (Jeffrey Hunter) throws dirt in his face.
b. his horse moves and he misses his shot.
c. he is shot in the shoulder with an arrow.

19. Who finally kills Chief Scar?

a. Ethan Edwards (John Wayne)
b. Martin Pauley (Jeffrey Hunter)
c. Debbie Edwards (Natalie Wood)

20. What does Ethan do when he finds Scar dead in his tent?

a. shoots his eyes out
b. scalps him
c. kicks him in the face

21. Ethan chases Debbie into a cave. What does he do to her?

a. he shoots her.
b. he takes her into his arms.
b. he slaps her face.

22. How many years did Ethan and Martin search for Debbie?

a. 2 years
b. 3 years
c. 5 years
d. 7 years

19

NUMBER TWO: RED RIVER

1. When Thomas Dunson (John Wayne) leaves the wagon train to search for land to start his ranch, he gives his girlfriend a token of his love until he would send for her. What did Dunson give her?

   a. a ring
   b. a bracelet
   c. a necklace

2. Why does Dunson get his bracelet back?

   a. His girlfriend marrys a rich banker and returns the bracelet.
   b. She dies of pneumonia and he takes it back before she dies.
   c. He takes it from the arm of an Indian brave he kills in a knife fight.

3. How many men did Dunson kill over the years protecting his ranch? The number of crosses in his cemetary was:

   a. three
   b. seven
   c. nine

4. At the beginning of the cattle drive, where is Dunson determined to take his cattle herd?

   a. Kansas
   b. Texas
   c. Missouri

5. When Dunson first meets young Matthew Garth, he is leading a cow. What else does he have with him?

   a. a bag of gold coins
   b. a small pistol
   c. a deed to land in Texas

6. Dunson takes Matthew with him and raises him like a son. What is the most important thing that Dunson teaches him?

   a. how to run a cattle ranch
   b. how to fast draw
   c. how to fight Indians

7. Why does Dunson have to take his cattle on a desperate cattle drive to Kansas?

   a. He wants to prove it can be done.
   b. The bank wants to foreclose on his ranch.
   c. Following the Civil War he is cash poor.

8. When Matt (Montgomery Cliff) first meets Cherry Valance they exchange guns and, to impress each other, they

   a. shoot the branches off a nearby tree
   b. shoot a tin can in the air
   c. shoot a silver dollar from a wagon wheel

9. During the cattle drive the herd is spooked into a stampede one night by what incident?

   a. a gun shot fired at a yowling coyote
   b. lightning striking a large tree
   c. pots and pans falling loudly from the chuckwagon.

10. How does Dunson want to punish the man responsible for the stampede?

    a. He wants to shoot him.
    b. He wants to whip him.
    c. He wants to hang him.

11. After the stampede conditions get rougher and the men talk about turning back. How does Dunson deal with this?

    a. He offers them large shares in the profits.
    b. He and Matt shoot the trouble makers.
    c. He stays awake at night watching them.

12. The final incident that forces Matt and the trail crew to take Dunson's herd away from him is:

    a. Dunson's heavy drinking
    b. Dunson wants to hang two runaways
    c. they run out of supplies

13. Which character is responsible for taking the herd away from Dunson?

    a. Cherry Valance
    b. Buster McGee
    c. Matthew Garth
    d. Dan Latimer

14. What advice does Dunson give Matt when he sets out to finish the cattle drive?

    a. Watch for Indians and border gangs.
    b. Watch behind you because one time I'll be there.
    c. Watch out for Cherry Valance.

15. Dunson follows after Matt and trails him to a wagon train. There he meets Tess who is in love with Matt. What does she attempt to do?

    a. poison his food
    b. shoot him while he's eating
    c. talk him out of killing Matt

16. Dunson meets Matt in the street but, before they can have their big showdown, he shoots it out with Cherry. Where is Dunson hit?

    a. in the right leg
    b. in the left hand
    c. in the left side
    d. in the right hand

17. Which cheek does Dunson graze when trying to get Matt to draw against him?

   a. left
   b. right

18. After the fist fight, Dunson and Matt reconcile and Dunson tells him to marry Tess and

   a. have plenty of children.
   b. change the branding irons when they get back to the ranch.
   c. learn how to fight like a man.

NUMBER THREE: SHE WORE A YELLOW RIBBON

1. Captain Nathan Brittles (John Wayne) is a career soldier about to be retired from the U.S. Cavalry. How long does he have left in the army at the start of the movie?

   a. two months
   b. two weeks
   c. six days

2. Captain Brittles tells us that he joined the Army as a poor bare-footed lad from what state?

   a. Iowa
   b. Indiana
   c. Ohio

3. Captain Brittles is a widower. What does he do to keep the memory of his wife alive?

   a. keeps her photograph on his desk
   b. has a new tombstone made
   c. visits her grave and talks with her

4. Captain Brittles' last military assignment is to:

   a. get the Indians back to the reservation.
   b. take a patrol to warn settlers while escorting the commandant's kin to the stagecoach stop.
   c. escort the army paymaster's stagecoach.

5. On the day of his retirement, the troop presents him with a gift. What did they give him?

   a. a new suit of civilian clothes
   b. a new horse and saddle
   c. a silver watch with inscription

6. Captain Brittles thinks his last mission was a failure, but in the final minutes of his military career he:

   a. captures two gun runners before they can sell repeating rifles to the Indians.
   b. captures the Indian chief before he can start the war.
   c. leads a surprise raid on the Indian camp to stampede their horses.

7. When Captain Brittles and Trooper Tyree enter the Indian camp to talk peace, a war chief who hates Brittles shoots an arrow at his feet. What does Brittles do?

   a. kicks the arrow in half
   b. breaks the arrow and spits on it
   c. ignores the arrow and the chief

8. Brittles rides off into the sunset but is chased down with a new set of orders. What do the orders say?

   a. he has been appointed commandant of the fort
   b. he has been appointed a Colonel
   c. he has been appointed Chief of Civilian Scouts

9. Where was Captain Brittles heading to retire?

   a. Indiana
   b. California
   c. Oregon

10. Brittles asked a favor from the commandant to keep Sgt. Quincannon in the guard house for two weeks for fighting. How many men did Quincannon fight?

    a. five
    b. six
    c. seven

11. What does Brittles do to Lt. Cohill (John Agar) that he had waited years for?

    a. turns over command of the troop
    b. calls him by his first name
    c. salutes him

12. The role as Nathan Brittles was significant for John Wayne because, for the first time:

    a. he dies in a film.
    b. he was directed by John Ford.
    c. he played a character older than himself.
    d. he was nominated for the Oscar.

13. Captain Brittles tells Miss Dandridge what it means in the cavalry when a woman wears a yellow ribbon. What does it mean?

    a. She is married to a trooper.
    b. She has a sweetheart in the cavalry.
    c. She is related to someone in the cavalry.

14. Who was the only general not to sign Captain Brittles new orders?

    a. General Grant
    b. General Sherman
    c. General Sheridan
    d. General Lee

15. When Captain Brittles arrives back at the fort and steps into the dance-hall, what is the first thing he does to Sgt. Quincannon?

a. shakes his hand
b. smells his breath
c. punches him in the mouth

16. Who played the role of Trooper Tyree?

a. John Agar
b. Harry Carey, Jr.
c. Ben Johnson

17. Who played the wounded trooper giving his report to Brittles?

a. Arthur Shields
b. Tom Tyler
c. George O'Brien

NUMBER FOUR: TRUE GRIT

1. Over which eye does Rooster Cogburn (John Wayne) wear his black eyepatch?

a. left
b. right

2. How did Rooster injure his eye?

a. during a bank robbery
b. during a civil war battle
c. in a gun fight

3. How many men did Rooster kill since becoming a "Peace Officer"?

a. 12
b. 19
c. 23

4. What was Rooster's big horse's name?

a. Buck
b. Old Dollar
c. Old Bo

5. What is his striped cat's name?

a. General Custer
b. General Sterling Price
c. General Robert E. Lee

6. What is the nickname that Rooster calls Mattie Ross (Kim Darby) during the film?

a. Little Britches
b. Baby Sister
c. Little Sister

7. Before he became a peace officer Rooster tried his hand at what?

   a. He owned a hardware store in New Mexico.
   b. He owned an eating place in Illinois.
   c. He mined gold in California.

8. Rooster tells Mattie that he once was married and that he also has a son. Their names are:

   a. Bond and Gillom
   b. Eula and Danny
   c. Nola and Horace

9. Rooster fought in the Civil War on the Confederate side. He admits to having rode with:

   a. General Jeb Stuart
   b. Capt. Charles Quantrill
   c. General Stonewall Jackson

10. Chaney, the man who Rooster and Mattie are searching for, joined the Ned Pepper gang. He is called Lucky Ned Pepper because Rooster once did what to him?

    a. shot his horse from under him
    b. gave him a five hour start to escape
    c. shot him in the lip

11. Rooster reluctantly joins forces with Le Boeff (Glen Campbell) to search for Tom Chaney. Le Boeff is also a peace officer. What rank is he?

    a. a deputy marshal
    b. a Texas ranger
    c. a town sheriff

12. In a bit of foreshadowing, Rooster tells Mattie something he once did against a posse. He does it later in the film. What is it?

    a. He jumps a horse over a fence.
    b. He stops drinking.
    c. He puts Bo's reins in his mouth and charges with both guns firing.

13. Ned Pepper makes Rooster angry by calling him a one-eyed, old fat man. What is Rooster's response?

    a. "I aim to kill you, Ned"
    b. "Fill your hand, you son of a bitch"
    c. "I'll see you hanged in Fort Smith"

14. Le Boeff saves Rooster's life twice, once by pulling him out of the snake pit. How did he help Rooster before?

    a. He shoots Tom Chaney before he can kill Rooster.
    b. He kills a rattlesnake about to strike Rooster.
    c. He kills Ned Pepper before he can shoot Rooster.

15. Mattie pays Rooster for capturing Chaney and she offers him a special gift. What does she want to give him?

    a. a new horse
    b. a place in her family cemetery plot
    c. $300 extra dollars

NUMBER FIVE: STAGECOACH

1. When the audience first sees the
   Ringo Kid, he is on foot and carrying
   what?

   a. his saddle and a rifle
   b. his saddle bag and a rifle
   c. his rifle and a water bag

2. The Kid busted out of territorial
   prison and is on his way to Lordsburg.
   Why?

   a. to find his girl and get married
   b. to get the man who stole his
      father's ranch
   c. to get the Plummer brothers who
      killed his father and brother

3. The Kid carried how many
   handguns?

   a. none
   b. one
   c. two

4. The Kid could have escaped before
   the stagecoach reaches Lordsburg.
   What keeps him with the stagecoach?

   a. He is in love with Dallas
      (Claire Trevor).
   b. He sees Apache smoke signals.
   c. He helps Doc Boone deliver a baby.

5. What was the name of the stage line?

   a. Wells Fargo
   b. Overland Stage Line
   c. Lordsburg Stage Line

6. What is special about the Ringo Kid's
   Winchester rifle?

   a. The barrel is sawed off.
   b. The arming lever has a round loop.

7. How many bullets does the Kid save
   and where does he hide the bullets?

   a. two bullets hidden in his boot
   b. three bullets hidden in his belt
   c. three bullets hidden in his hat

8. The Kid goes up against the
   Plummer brothers. How many
   brothers does he face and how many
   do we see die?

   a. two brothers, none seen dying
   b. three brothers, one dies in the bar
   c. four brothers, three die in the street

9. The Kid fell in love with Dallas but
   didn't know she was thrown out of
   town for being a(n):

   a. card cheat
   b. alcoholic
   c. prostitute

10. After taking care of the Plummer
    brothers, what happens to the Kid
    and Dallas?

    a. He is taken to jail and she waits for
       him.
    b. He goes to jail and she goes to his
       ranch.
    c. They ride off in a buckboard to his
       ranch.

11. Stagecoach was John Wayne's vehicle to "A" Movies and Super Stardom. Yet, The Duke thought another actor would be good in the role of the Ringo Kid. What actor did Wayne have in mind?

a. Gary Cooper
b. Lloyd Nolan
c. Joel McCrea
d. Randolph Scott

12. Stagecoach was only the second western ever nominated for the Academy Award. Stagecoach lost the Oscar for best picture to what film?

a. The Wizard of Oz
b. Wuthering Heights
c. Gone With The Wind

13. Stagecoach did win an Oscar for best supporting actor. The actor was:

a. John Carradine
b. Thomas Mitchell
c. Andy Devine

14. A member of the Stagecoach cast fathered three sons who went on to become actors. His name is:

a. John Wayne
b. John Carradine
c. Lloyd Bridges

15. The location for most of Stagecoach was filmed in a part of the United States that has since become known as John Ford territory. The location was:

a. Death Valley, Utah
b. Grants Pass, Oregon
c. Monument Valley, Arizona/Utah

16. Who wrote the short story that Stagecoach was based on?

a. Zane Grey
b. Ernest Haycox
c. Ernest Hemingway

NUMBER SIX: THE SHOOTIST

1. Aging gunfighter John Bernard Books (John Wayne) comes to visit Dr. Hosetler (Jimmy Stewart) to confirm what?

a. that he is slowly going blind.
b. that he is dying of cancer.
c. that he has a fatal heart condition.

2. Dr. Hosetler tells him what to expect and recommends a local boarding house to stay in. Books lies about his identity and tells the landlady (Lauren Bacall) that he is a peace officer named:

a. Bat Masterson
b. Wyatt Earp
c. William Hickok

3. Mrs. Rogers' son Gillom learns Books true identity. How?

   a. The town marshal tells him.
   b. Dr. Hosetler tells him.
   c. Moses the stable owner finds his name on his saddle.
   d. His mother tells him.

4. What did J.B. Books buy his first day in town?

   a. a tombstone
   b. a newspaper
   c. a new suit
   d. a new pocket watch

5. While laying in his bed, Books hears a noise outside his bedroom window. He gets out of bed and waits. When the shooting stops how many men did he kill?

   a. two
   b. three
   c. four

6. Gillom (Ron Howard) admires Books even more after the attempt on his life. What does he ask Books to do for him?

   a. sell him his horse
   b. let him run errands for him
   c. give him a shooting lesson

7. Books makes a statement about gunfighting to Gillom that fore-shadows his own death when he says:

   a. You have to kill without hesitation.
   b. You have to watch for the amateur.
   c. You need two guns.

8. Books sells his horse for the money. What is his horse's name?

   a. Old Yellow
   b. Old Bo
   c. Old Dollar

9. Books' old girlfriend comes to visit him and asks him to do what?

   a. allow her to write a book about his life
   b. marry her so she can earn money as his widow
   c. lend her enough money to go to Denver

10. Books gets a haircut and while in the barbershop makes arrangements for what?

   a. to purchase birthday presents
   b. the sale of his horse and saddle
   c. his funeral and tombstone

The Duke as Ethan Edwards in The Searchers his greatest role.

John Ford had such confidence in the Duke's ability to play the part of the Ringo Kid that he refused to make the film without Wayne in the role. Ford finally convinced Walter Wanger to produce the film with Wayne in the lead.

The Duke's first wife was the daughter of a Panamanian diplomat. Duke married Josephine Saenz in 1933. They had four children and were divorced in 1945. Actress Loretta Young was maid of honor at their wedding. The first Mrs. Wayne never remarried and always used the name of Morrison.

The Duke's second wife was a some-time Mexican actress named Esperanza Diaz Ceballos Baur. Her nickname was Chata which meant Pugnose in Spanish. They were married in 1946 and divorced in 1953.

The Duke's second wife Chata was once married to a man named Eugene Morrison before she wed The Duke in 1946.

The Duke was married to his third wife Pilar Palette on November 1, 1954. She was 25 years younger than the Duke when they married and was a Peruvian actress. They separated in 1973.

The Duke's most quoted comment on his acting is: "I don't act, I react."

The Duke was an avid chess player and carried a small chess set with him so that he could play at a moment's notice.

11. Books invites three men to the local saloon to face him on his birthday. One of the three knows him from the past. Mike Sweeney (Richard Boone) had a special reason for coming. What was the reason?

   a. Books had killed his father.
   b. Books had sent him to prison.
   c. Books had killed his brother.

12. Before he leaves his room two workers bring his newly cut tombstone. If you read the dates you would see that John Bernard Books was how old?

   a. 58
   b. 62
   c. 66

13. What did Books leave in his room for Mrs. Rogers?

   a. a farewell letter
   b. his gold watch and money
   c. the bill of sale for his horse

14. Who fatally shoots Books during the gunfight?

   a. the town Marshal
   b. the town gambler
   c. the bartender

NUMBER SEVEN: THE QUIET MAN

1. What is Sean Thornton (Wayne) holding in his hand after he steps from the train?

   a. a fishing pole
   b. a sleeping bag
   c. an apple

2. What is Sean Thornton's former occupation, and why did he give it up?

   a. He was in oil and made a fortune.
   b. He was a professional boxer who killed someone in a fight.
   c. He was a coal miner who saved his money to retire.

3. Where in America did Sean live before returning home to Ireland?

   a. Pittsburgh
   b. Boston
   c. Chicago

4. What is the reason Sean has returned to Ireland?

   a. to meet his relatives
   b. to find a wife
   c. to buy his family cottage to live in
   d. to buy a race horse.

5. Where does Sean first see Mary Kate Danaher played by Maureen O'Hara?

   a. kneeling in church praying
   b. in an open field herding her sheep
   c. riding her bicycle

6. Sean unwittingly becomes an enemy of Red Will Danaher when he does what?

   a. befriends the wealthy widow
   b. beats him in a horse race
   c. outbids him for his family cottage
   d. asks for his sister's hand in marriage

7. Sean wants to marry Mary Kate but Red Will refuses to allow it until what happens?

   a. Sean agrees to pay Mary Kate's dowry.
   b. Sean wins the local horse race.
   c. Will thinks he will be able to marry the rich widow.
   c. The local priest threatens to excommunicate him.

8. Sean and Mary Kate court and finally marry. What happens on their wedding day?

   a. Sean is knocked out by Red Will.
   b. Will refuses to give Mary Kate her dowry.
   c. Sean and Mary Kate quarrel in their cottage.
   d. all of the above.

9. Why is Sean afraid to confront and fight Red Will?

   a. He is afraid of him.
   b. He killed a boxer in a fight.
   c. He promised his wife he wouldn't fight.

10. What finally gets Sean mad enough to fight Red Will Danaher?

   a. Danaher shames him at the local pub.
   b. His wife makes him walk home from a shopping trip.
   c. Mary Kate leaves him early in the morning.

11. Where does Sean catch up with Mary Kate?

   a. She is hiding in church.
   b. She is hiding in a railroad car.
   c. She is hiding in her brother's house.

12. What does Sean do when he finds Mary Kate?

   a. puts her on his horse and takes her home
   b. walks her back to her brother's farm
   c. takes her to the local priest

13. Sean demands Mary Kate's dowry from her brother. How much money does Will owe Sean?

   a. 250 pounds
   b. 350 pounds
   c. 500 pounds

14. What does Sean do with the money when he gets it from Danaher?

   a. offers to buy everyone drinks
   b. throws it into a fire
   c. gives it to the town priest

15. Sean finally fights Red Will. How does the fight end?

   a. The local priest stops it.
   b. The IRA stops it.
   c. Sean knocks Will through a pub door.
   d. Will knocks Sean into a brook.

NUMBER EIGHT: RIO GRANDE

1. How does Lt. Colonel Kirby Yorke (John Wayne) learn that his son is in the cavalry?

   a. He reads his name on the new recruit list.
   b. His wife arrives in camp and tells him.
   c. He hears his name called at inspection.

2. Why did Jeff Yorke join the cavalry?

   a. He wanted to be like his father.
   b. He failed mathematics at West Point.
   c. His mother made him join the Army.

3. What does Col. Yorke tell his son when they first meet in his tent?

   a. He should request a transfer to another post.
   b. He is pleased that he joined the Army.
   c. He will expect twice as much from him.

4. Mrs. Yorke arrives unexpectedly at the post. What does she want from her husband?

   a. She wants a divorce.
   b. She wants to get her son back into West Point.
   c. She wants her son released from the army.

5. The Yorke's have been apart for many years. What is the reason they separated?

   a. Kirby fought on the Union Side.
   b. Kirby ordered her plantation burned.
   c. Kirby accidently killed her brother.

6. How many years have Col. Yorke and his wife been separated?

   a. eight
   b. ten
   c. fifteen

7. What was the name of Mrs. Yorke's plantation?

   a. Tara
   b. Brideshead
   c. Bridesdale

8. When Mrs. Yorke first sees Sgt. Major Quincannon (Victor McLaglen) what does she call him?

   a. a drunkard
   b. an arsonist
   c. a damn yankee

9. At a dinner in her honor, Mrs. Yorke is serenaded by the regimental singers. What song do they sing for her?

   a. My Old Kentucky Home
   b. I'll Take You Home Again, Kathleen
   c. The Yellow Rose of Texas

10. In a moment of tenderness between them, what does Kirby Yorke show his wife that he has kept as a sentimental remembrance?

    a. his wedding band
    b. her photo in a locket
    c. a Confederate ten dollar bill

11. What Union Army general arrives at the post to talk with Kirby Yorke about the Indian situation?

    a. General Grant
    b. General Sherman
    c. General Sheridan

12. What orders does Yorke get "off the record?"

    a. Don't take any Indian prisoners
    b. Chase the Apaches into Mexico
    c. Get back together with his wife

13. Col. Yorke sends three men on a dangerous mission, one of them is his son. What is their mission?

    a. locate the Apache camp
    b. stampede the Apache's horses
    c. locate and defend the kidnapped children

14. What happens to Col. Yorke when he leads the attack against the Apaches?

    a. He is shot in the leg with a bullet.
    b. He is shot in the shoulder with an arrow.
    c. He is hit in the back with a lance.

15. At the award ceremony following the successful battle against the Apaches, what happens out of the ordinary?

    a. The Indian scouts get medals.
    b. The colonel's son is made an officer.
    c. The army band plays Dixie.

NUMBER NINE: SANDS OF IWO JIMA

1. When we first meet Sgt. John Stryker (Wayne), he is a platoon sergeant with three stripes. What rank was he before?

   a. Sergeant Major
   b. Master Sergeant
   c. Lieutenant

2. Why was Stryker demoted?

   a. He hit an enlisted man.
   b. He was found drunk.
   c. He was caught gambling.

3. One of the new men in Stryker's platoon knows him from the past. Why did Cpl. Al Thomas (Forrest Tucker) hate Stryker?

   a. Stryker had him demoted.
   b. Stryker stole his wife from him.
   c. Stryker beat him in a boxing match.

4. The one recruit who Stryker has the hardest time getting to know is Pete Conway (John Agar). Stryker knew what member of Conway's family?

   a. his brother
   b. his father
   c. his uncle

5. Why did Conway, who hates both Stryker and the Corps, join the Marines?

   a. He had to prove he wasn't a coward.
   b. His father was a Marine officer.
   c. It was a family tradition.

6. Stryker is tough on his men. He busts a left-handed marine on the jaw to teach him how to use his bayonet the right way. What does he finally do to get the marine to learn how to fight with the bayonet?

   a. He takes away his three day pass.
   b. He makes him practice to a polka recording.
   c. He gives him extra training.

7. How does Stryker call his platoon into action?

   a. "Lock and load."
   b. "Hit the deck."
   c. "Saddle up."

8. What island did Stryker's platoon first see combat on?

   a. Guadalcanal
   b. Tarawa
   c. Iwo Jima

9. Stryker saves Conway's life. How does he do it?

   a. He shoots a Jap about to bayonet him.
   b. He pushes him aside from a landmine.
   c. He knocks him to the ground as a grenade explodes.

10. Stryker and Thomas finally have a fistfight. What are they fighting about?

    a. Stryker learned that Thomas was a coward.
    b. Stryker learned that Thomas got one of his men killed.
    c. Thomas tells Stryker he's had it with him.

11. Stryker is a hard drinker off duty. What is he drinking to forget?

    a. that he was demoted.
    b. that he is afraid of combat.
    c. that his wife left him and took their son.

12. When Stryker is picked up in a bar and goes home with the woman, he surprises her and himself by:

    a. falling asleep on her couch
    b. giving her money for her baby
    c. cooking her dinner

13. How does Stryker meet his destiny on Iwo Jima?

    a. He is killed trying to blow up a pill-box.
    b. He is bayoneted in a foxhole.
    c. He is shot to death by a sniper.

14. Which one of Stryker's men reads the unfinished letter to his son?

    a. John Agar
    b. Forrest Tucker
    c. James Brown

15. What are the Marines doing at the time of Stryker's death?

    a. Raising the flag on Mount Suribachi
    b. Attacking the beachhead
    c. Retreating down the mountain

NUMBER TEN: THREE GODFATHERS

1. When Robert Marmaduke Hightower (John Wayne) first meets the local Marshal (Ward Bond) he laughs at him. Why?

   a. He has a funny sounding first name.
   b. His wife is making a fuss over him.
   c. He falls off his horse.

2. What are Hightower and his two friends in town for?

   a. to buy some cattle
   b. to rob the bank
   c. to buy some horses

3. Hightower's plans to cross the local desert are spoiled by Marshal Sweet. What does the Marshal do?

   a. shoots one of the three horses
   b. blows up the nearest water well
   c. shoots a hole in their water bag

4. Forced to cross the desert, the trio are slowed down by the lack of water and:

   a. the lack of food
   b. the wounded Abilene Kid
   c. a crippled horse

5. The three outlaws reach the first water hole. What do they find there?

   a. a dry hole
   b. a band of Indians
   c. a group of deputies

6. Traveling again through the desert, they finally reach the second source of water. What do they find this time?

   a. the burned remains of a wagon train
   b. plenty of well water
   c. a pregnant woman in a covered wagon

7. Hightower is the smart tough leader of the trio but what is he afraid of?

   a. dying of thirst in the desert
   b. helping the woman have the baby
   c. spending the rest of his life in prison

8. Which one of the bandits helps deliver the baby?

   a. Hightower
   b. The Mexican
   c. The Abilene Kid

9. When the baby is born, why is he given the first name of Robert?

   a. It was his father's name.
   b. Hightower was the first to find the mother.
   c. The three outlaws drew straws for the names.

10. The three godfathers decide to try to save their godson and walk to the nearest town. What is the name of the town?

   a. Bethlehem
   b. Last Chance
   c. New Jerusalem
   d. Welcome

11. Which one of the three godfathers lives and saves the baby?

    a. John Wayne
    b. Pedro Armendariz
    c. Harry Carey, Jr.

12. The baby's natural kin turns out to be who?

    a. the owner of the bank
    b. the town Marshal
    c. the town Judge

13. Hightower gets a reduced prison sentence because:

    a. he saved the baby's life.
    b. he returned the bank's money.
    c. he refused to break his promise to the baby's mother.

14. On what holiday does Hightower arrive in town?

    a. New Year's Eve
    b. Christmas
    c. Easter

15. The movie Three Godfathers was dedicated to an old-time cowboy star who starred in an earlier version of the story. His son had a part in the film. The son was:

    a. Noah Berry, Jr.
    b. Claude Jarman, Jr.
    c. Harry Carey, Jr.

Two of the Duke's children from his marriage to Pilar Palette were born on the same day, four years apart. John Ethan Wayne was born on February 22, 1962, and his sister Marisa Carmela Wayne was born on February 22, 1966.

The Duke's children from two of his marriages have appeared with their father in a total of ten John Wayne films.

A young John Wayne played an harmonica in the 1933 "B" western called The Telegraph Trail.

In the years on Poverty Row making "B" and "C" films before Stagecoach, The Duke appeared with such future stars as Barbara Stanwyck, Loretta Young, Jennifer Jones, Mickey Rooney, Pat O'Brien and Dick Powell.

The Duke appeared in two 1935 "B" westerns with none other than Buffalo Bill, Jr. The movies were Texas Terror and Rainbow Valley.

One of The Duke's early childhood heros was Harry Carey, Sr. They made four films together. Three Godfathers which is considered a minor classic is dedicated to Harry Carey.

The Duke's locations for many of his westerns was Mexico. In his honor, the international airport in Durango, Mexico is named after him.

The Duke was an honor student in both high school and college. He once said they had to teach him to say "ain't" when he began his career in films.

The Duke as cavalry officer Kirby Yorke a character he played in two films Fort Apache and Rio Grande.

CHAPTER THREE

THE DUKE ON FILM...THE MINOR CLASSICS

The following John Wayne films rank right behind his ten best screen performances and represent work that continued to demonstrate his screen presence, acting ability, and strong box office appeal. Most of the films in this group show Wayne as the mature superstar in a variety of action settings. These films are solid, vintage John Wayne and should be watched whenever they are shown. They are ranked below followed by trivia questions from each film.

RANK	MOVIE TITLE	YEAR MADE
11	They Were Expendable	1945
12	Fort Apache	1948
13	The Man Who Shot Liberty Valance	1962
14	Rio Bravo	1959
15	The Horse Soldiers	1959
16	North to Alaska	1960
17	The Comancheros	1961
18	The Wings of Eagles	1957
19	Reap the Wild Wind	1942
20	The Long Voyage Home	1948

NUMBER ELEVEN: THEY WERE EXPENDABLE

1. As the title of this film suggests, during the early months of World War II, many American fighting men were expendable. The period of the War that formed the backdrop for this John Wayne war film was:

   a. the attack on Pearl Harbor
   b. the battle of Midway
   c. the fall of the Philippines

2. What is Lt. Rusty Ryan (John Wayne) doing at the time they announce the attack on Pearl Harbor?

   a. He is announcing his engagement.
   b. He is filling out his transfer papers.
   c. He is talking with the fleet admiral.

3. What type of ships did Rusty and his fellow officers command?

   a. P-T boats
   b. Destroyers
   c. Submarines

4. Rusty Ryan was second-in-command to John Brickley, played in the film by a returning naval veteran. Who had the starring role in this film?

   a. Henry Fonda
   b. James Stewart
   c. Robert Montgomery
   d. Tyrone Power

5. All the men are anxious to get into combat. What is the crew's first assignment:

   a. transporting troops between the islands
   b. transporting messages for the admiral
   c. attacking Japanese ships

6. Rusty misses the first major combat mission. Why?

   a. His ship is sunk during an air attack.
   b. He is assigned to desk duty.
   c. His wounded hand becomes infected.

7. Rusty meets a Navy nurse and they fall in love. The young lady in later life had a television series. Lt. Sandy Davyss is played by:

   a. Barbara Bel Geddes
   b. Donna Reed
   c. Gale Storm
   d. Elizabeth Montgomery

8. Brickley and Rusty get to transport a noted historical figure in the film. Name the person they transport.

   a. Harry S. Truman
   b. Fleet Admiral Nimetz
   c. General Douglas A. MacArthur
   d. General James E. Doolittle

9. After several battles with the Japanese, what happens to Rusty's ship?

   a. It is sunk by a Jap airplane.
   b. It is sunk by a Jap submarine.
   c. It is stripped and blown up.

10. Brickley and Rusty are ready to continue fighting the Japanese on land but what happens to them?

    a. They are captured by the Japs.
    b. They are ordered to escape by submarine.
    c. They are flown out to the States.
    d. They are killed in combat.

11. How many boats in Motor Torpedo Squadron No. 3?

    a. two
    b. four
    c. six

12. How is Rusty wounded?

    a. Rusty's right hand is hit during a Jap air attack.
    b. Rusty is wounded when his ship is sunk.
    c. Rusty is shot through both ankles by the Japs.

13. How does young nurse Sandy Davyss impress Rusty?

   a. She orders him into bed.
   b. She tells him to shut his mouth in the hospital.
   c. She throws a blanket over him and pulls off his pants.

14. In a romantic scene at a dance, Sandy and Rusty tell each other what states they each are from. Where are they from?

   a. Sandy is from California and Rusty is from Iowa.
   b. Sandy is from Iowa and Rusty is from New York.
   c. Sandy is from Indiana and Rusty is from Maine.

15. At the very end, Rusty tries to leave the last airplane sent to fly him off the island. Why?

   a. He wants to stay with his ship's crew.
   b. He wants to stay to find Sandy.
   c. He wants to give his place to a married pilot.

NUMBER TWELVE: FORT APACHE

1. Capt. Kirby York (Wayne) is relieved from command by Lt. Col. Owen Thursday (Henry Fonda). What is the new commandant's main character trait?

   a. He lives only by the rules.
   b. He has a good sense of humor.
   c. He is unable to make a decision.
   d. He dislikes enlisted men.

2. Lt. Col. Thursday's daughter in the film was played by a well known child star. Her name is:

   a. Ann Rutherford
   b. Judy Garland
   c. Shirley Temple
   d. Margaret O'Brien

3. Miss Thursday had a very unusual first name. Her name in the movie was:

   a. Prudence
   b. Providence
   c. Philadelphia
   d. Chasity

4. Although Lt. Col. Thursday has other ideas, he sends Capt. York to Cochise's camp. Why does York go?

   a. to get Cochise to sign a peace treaty
   b. to ask Cochise to return to the reservation
   c. to request return of kidnapped children
   d. to ask Cochise to attend a pow-wow

5. Cochise agrees to meet with Thursday. What does Thursday do that upsets York?

   a. He orders the entire garrison to march.
   b. He insults Cochise and orders him back to the government reservation.
   c. He threatens Cochise with imprisonment.

6. Thursday's contempt for the Indians leads to what?

   a. his great victory and a promotion
   b. disgrace to the command
   c. his ultimate death

7. York is spared the fate of Thursday and most of the troop. Why?

   a. He argues with Thursday regarding the Indians fighting habits.
   b. He is called a coward and relieved of duty.
   c. He is wounded and sent to the rear for aid.
   d. He is sent to guard the supply wagons in the rear.

8. Capt. York's relationship with Cochise was based on what?

   a. York could speak his language.
   b. York once saved his life.
   c. York had never lied to him.

9. After the fatal battle Cochise rides up to York and does what?

   a. He spits in his face.
   b. He throws the cavalry regimental standard at his feet and rides away.
   c. He shoots an arrow at his feet and rides away.
   d. He calls him a false friend and declares war on the cavalry.

10. York later becomes commandant and while discussing the troops famous battle with newsmen does what?

   a. He agrees with their version of the events.
   b. He agrees to tell them the truth regarding Thursday.
   c. He lies about how the troops and Thursday died.

NUMBER THIRTEEN: THE MAN WHO SHOT LIBERTY VALANCE

1. How do Tom Doniphon (Wayne) and Stoddard (James Stewart) meet in the film?

   a. Tom finds Stoddard beaten and half dead.
   b. Stoddard is working in a restaurant.
   c. They meet at a political convention.

2. Doniphon saves Stoddards life and finds his ideas on law and order amusing. What nickname does Tom give him?

   a. "Baby Brother"
   b. "Dude"
   c. "Pilgrim"
   d. "Tenderfoot"

The Duke as gunfighter Quirt Evans about to shoot it out in the street. The film is Angel and the Badman, the first film that Wayne produced.

John Wayne movie buffs should know that the Duke appeared in three 12-part serials. They were Shadow of the Eagle, The Hurricane Express, and The Three Musketeers. The Duke also appeared in a series of eight films playing Stony Brooke, one of the Three Mesquiteers.

The Duke's lifelong friend Yakima Canutt who appeared in 20 films with Wayne is best remembered for doubling for Wayne as the Ringo Kid in Stagecoach. It was Canutt who performed the dangerous stunt where the Ringo Kid rides atop the horse team to retrieve the loose horse reins. A magic moment in film history.

The Duke along with Yakima Canutt perfected the horsefall and other riding tricks that appear in most westerns today.

John Wayne often admitted that he borrowed his famous walk and talk from his life long friend stuntman Yakima Canutt.

The Duke is credited with bringing realism to the western film. He broke the stereotype that the hero had to be dressed in white. The Duke dressed as real cowboys would dress and even started the practice where the good guy threw the first punch in a fight.

The Duke loved the sea. The names of the boats that he owned over the years were: Apache, Isthmus, Nor'wester and Wild Goose II.

John Ford is godfather to The Duke's second son, Patrick John Wayne.

3. The first time we see Doniphon face off against the evil Liberty Valance, they nearly shoot it out. Why?

    a. Liberty insulted Tom's girl Hallie.
    b. Liberty trips Stoddard who drops Tom's steak.
    c. Liberty tries to break up an election meeting.

4. How does Stoddard recognize Valance as the man who robbed the stage and whipped him?

    a. from his voice and boots
    b. from the guns he wears
    c. from the whip he carries

5. What is Ranse Stoddard's real occupation?

    a. He is a politician.
    b. He is a school teacher.
    c. He is a lawyer.
    d. He is a newspaper editor.

6. Doniphon protects Stoddard for a while, then Liberty tells him to leave town or meet him in the street. How does Stoddard prepare for the showdown?

    a. He asks Tom to shoot it out with Liberty.
    b. Tom gives him some shooting lessons.
    c. He sends for the territorial marshal.

7. Valance hates Stoddard. What name does he call him?

    a. Carpetbagger
    b. Dude
    c. Pilgrim

8. In the final showdown between Liberty and Stoddard, what happens?

    a. Liberty shoots Stoddard in the leg.
    b. Pompey shoots Liberty in the head.
    c. Tom shoots and kills Liberty from the alley.

9. When Tom finally realizes that Hallie is in love with Stoddard, what does he do?

    a. He gets drunk and clears out the bar.
    b. He gets drunk and burns his ranch house.
    c. He sells his ranch and leaves town.

10. Stoddard becomes a town hero after Liberty's death but refuses to go into politics. What changes his mind?

    a. The town newspaper editor convinces him.
    b. Hallie tells him to do it for her.
    c. Tom tells him it was he who shot Liberty.

11. All but one of these well known
   Hollywood heavies were members of
   Liberty Valance's gang. Name the
   good guy.

   a. Strother Martin
   b. Jack Elam
   c. Woody Strode
   d. Lee Van Cleef

NUMBER FOURTEEN: RIO BRAVO

1. When Rio Bravo starts, John T.
   Chance (Wayne) is bleeding from a
   head wound. Who hit him?

   a. the young town gunfighter
   b. the brother of the rich cattleman
   c. his former deputy
   d. his new girlfriend

2. Why did Chance and Dude (Dean
   Martin) fight?

   a. Chance tried to stop him from
      drinking.
   b. Chance tried to stop him from
      getting a dollar out of a spittoon.
   c. Dude hates Chance for firing him.
   d. Chance tried to arrest him for
      cheating at poker.

3. We learn that Dude was once
   Chance's deputy until something
   happened to him. What turned Dude
   into the town drunk?

   a. He accidentally shot and killed
      a child.
   b. He was seriously wounded in the
      Civil War.
   c. He fell in love with a bad woman.

4. What is the name of the old deputy
   back in the jailhouse?

   a. Gabby
   b. Colorado
   c. Stumpy
   d. Pappy

5. After Chance arrests Joe Burdette,
   how many deputies does he have to
   guard the jail?

   a. one
   b. two
   c. three

6. An old friend of Chance's comes to
   town leading a small wagon train.
   What actor played the small role of
   Pat Wheeler, the old friend who
   wanted to help?

   a. Walter Brennan
   b. Ward Bond
   c. John Russell

7. What happens to prevent Pat Wheeler from helping Chance guard his prisoner?

   a. He is beaten and leaves town.
   b. Chance tells him to stay out of his affairs.
   c. He is shot in back by a paid killer.
   d. He receives a telegram and leaves town.

8. Chance and Dude chase a hired killer into a bar. How does Dude identify him before killing him?

   a. by the new $20 dollar gold coin in his pocket
   b. by the blood dripping on the bar from a leg wound
   c. by the mud on his boots
   d. by his horse tied outside the bar

9. How does Chance express his anger at the Burdette gang for killing his friend Pat Wheeler?

   a. takes their guns and orders them out of town
   b. shoots three of the gang
   c. hits a gang member in the face with his rifle

10. With all his problems in holding Joe Burdette, Chance also becomes involved with a woman passing through town. What is her nickname?

   a. High Pockets
   b. Feathers
   c. Dallas

11. What is it that Chance always carried with him?

   a. a bowie knife
   b. a small pistol in his boot
   c. a loaded Winchester rifle

12. When Chance is captured and Dude kidnapped, who saves the day?

   a. the owner of the hotel
   b. Chance's girlfriend
   c. the old deputy
   d. the young gunfighter

13. During a break in the action, the deputies sing an old western song. What is the name of the song?

   a. Don't Fence Me In
   b. Wagon Wheels
   c. Get Along Cindy
   d. Yellow Rose of Texas

14. Chance has to swap Joe Burdette for Dude. In the final showdown, not only does he re-arrest Joe, he captures the entire Burdette gang. How does The Duke do it?

   a. A group of federal marshals arrive to help.
   b. Some old civil war buddies form a posse.
   c. He uses dynamite to get them to surrender.

15. At the film's end, Chance threatens to arrest his girlfriend. Why?

    a. He sees her likeness on a Wanted poster.
    b. He catches her cheating at poker.
    c. She wants to work as a bar girl.
    d. She puts on a sexy costume.

NUMBER FIFTEEN: THE HORSE SOLDIERS

1. In The Horse Soldiers what did John Marlowe (Wayne) do in civilian life before becoming a Colonel in the Union Army?

    a. He was a cattle rancher.
    b. He was a railroad engineer.
    c. He was a doctor.
    d. He was a mining engineer.

2. What is Col. Marlowe's secret mission?

    a. to attack Andersonville prison
    b. to destroy a major Confederate railway junction
    c. to surround Gen. Lee's remaining forces

3. Major Kendall the military surgeon assigned to Marlowe's command was played by a popular leading man of the time. He was:

    a. Glenn Ford
    b. Richard Egan
    c. William Holden
    d. Robert Mitchum

4. Col. Marlowe and Major Kendall dislike each other from the start. Why are they at odds with each other?

    a. Kendall knows that Marlowe is not a West Point graduate.
    b. Kendall is too soft on the troops.
    c. They have different views on how to treat the troops.
    d. They are in love with the same woman.

5. Later in the film we learn why Marlowe has a personal dislike for Kendall. What is the reason?

    a. Marlowe dislikes all West Point graduates.
    b. Marlowe hates all surgeons since his wife died after surgery.
    c. Marlowe resents Kendall's interference with his command.

6. The two officers refer to each other in un-gentlemanly terms. What does Marlowe call Kendall?

    a. butcher
    b. croaker
    c. blood sucker

7. The Union troops are discovered by a rebel patrol. What does Col. Marlowe do?

   a. He retreats back to Vicksburg.
   b. He attacks the small Confederate force.
   c. He splits his troops sending one-third back.
   d. He continues on his mission without change.

8. Why does The Duke have to bring Miss Hannah Hunter along on his military mission?

   a. She is a northern spy.
   b. She is a southern spy.
   c. She falls in love with him.
   d. He falls in love with her.

9. Kendall shows less than proper respect for his commanding officer. He calls Marlowe what?

   a. old iron head
   b. section hand
   c. yard bird

10. After destroying the Confederate rail town, what southern city do the Union troops plan to reach for safety?

    a. New Orleans
    b. Atlanta
    c. Vicksburg
    d. Baton Rogue

11. What is the name of the plantation that the Union troops spend the night at?

    a. Tara
    b. Bridesdale
    c. Greenbriar

12. If you watch closely during the film, the face of old sergeant appears in several scenes. This actor was an old time cowboy star. His name is:

    a. Tom Tyler
    b. Hoot Gibson
    c. Bob Steele
    d. Tex Ritter

13. Col. Marlowe shows his good side to the southern lady who is traveling with his command when he does what?

    a. frees a group of black slaves
    b. does not burn down her family plantation
    c. frees an old sheriff from two Rebel deserters

14. The southern belle in the film was played by an actress who later in real life was married to the American Ambassador to Mexico. Her name is:

    a. Angie Dickinson
    b. Constance Towers
    c. Tippi Hendron
    d. Marie Windsor

15. In a scene intended to project some humor, what does Col. Marlowe order his trooper to do with a captured Confederate military schoolboy?

   a. punch him in the mouth
   b. give him a drink of bourbon
   c. spank him then set him free

16. Col. Marlowe is wounded before the final battle. Where is he hit?

   a. He is shot in the arm.
   b. He is shot in the side.
   c. He is shot in the lower leg.
   d. He is shot in the shoulder.

17. Marlowe gains enough time for his troops to escape. Before he leaves Kendall and the wounded behind, how do we know that he has fallen for the southern belle?

   a. He gives her a bracelet.
   b. He places her bandanna around his neck.
   c. He gives her his military class ring.
   d. He tells her he's fallen in love with her.

NUMBER SIXTEEN: NORTH TO ALASKA

1. When we first meet Sam McCord (Wayne), he is talking about the trip he is taking to Seattle. Sam is going to buy mining equipment. What else is he going to Seattle for?

   a. to buy guns to protect the mine
   b. to hire workers to work the mine
   c. to escort his partner's fiancée Jenny back to Alaska
   d. to buy gifts for his partner's wedding

2. Sam McCord's partner is George Pratt. The actor who played this role made only a few westerns in his career. The actor was?

   a. Robert Taylor
   b. Kirk Douglas
   c. Stewart Granger
   d. George Montgomery

3. Sam and George have a long bar brawl to defend Jenny's honor. When it's over, Sam goes to the Turkish bath. Here he meets a crooked gambler named Frankie Canon. Who played the role of Frankie?

   a. Jackie Cooper
   b. Ernie Kovacs
   c. Denver Pyle
   d. George Kennedy

4. Sam punches Frankie soon after they meet. Why?

   a. Frankie tried to steal Sam's suitcase filled with money.
   b. Frankie tried to pick Sam's pocket.
   c. Frankie tried to sell Sam a phoney diamond ring.
   d. Frankie said something bad about George Pratt.

5. When Sam arrives in Seattle, he visits Jenny and learns that she is already married. What does he do?

   a. He gets drunk and takes the ship back to Alaska.
   b. He goes to a lumberjack picnic.
   c. He asks a French callgirl to come back to Alaska with him.
   d. He wires George the bad news.

6. Before leaving Seattle what else does Sam do?

   a. He enters a beer drinking contest.
   b. He enters a tree climbing contest.
   c. He enters an ax throwing contest.
   d. He enters a log rolling contest.

7. Back at the mine is little Billy Pratt, George's kid brother. In one of his best screen performances, this person was not known for his acting. What was he in real life?

   a. He was a football star.
   b. He was a former war hero.
   c. He was a rock and roll singer.
   d. He was a Broadway actor.

8. George is angry with Sam for not bringing Jenny back with him. He then meets Michelle and likes the idea of a substitute French woman. What happens to change his mind?

   a. Brother Billy falls in love with her.
   b. George realizes that Sam loves her.
   c. She falls in love with Frankie.

9. Sam and George's troubles increase when they learn that someone has filed a cross-claim against their gold mine. Who played the town drunk Boggs who filed the cross-claim?

   a. Red Buttons
   b. Chill Wills
   c. Mickey Shaughnessy
   d. Joe Sawyer

10. All ends well when Sam fights the real crook Frankie and saves his mine. Michelle has a ticket to sail to Seattle. How does Sam keep her in Alaska?

   a. He gives her half of the mine.
   b. He tells her he loves her.
   c. He buys her Frankie's saloon.

11. Sam gives Angel (Michelle) a ring to show that he really loves her. Who gave Sam the ring?

   a. Frankie
   b. Billy
   c. George

The Duke as Hondo Lane from the film Hondo made in 1953.

Film Historians credit John Wayne and legendary stuntman Yakima Canutt with inventing and perfecting the modern screen fight. Together Duke and Yak perfected the "near-miss" and other camera techniques associated with making screen fights look so realistic.

The best known fight scene The Duke was involved in was not in a western but in the Irish love story The Quiet Man. In this film, Duke and Victor McLaglen brawled for eight minutes and 53 seconds, making it one of the longest screen fights ever filmed.

The movie that changed the Duke's life and film career Stagecoach started out as a short story by Ernest Haycox in Collier's Magazine entitled The Stage to Lordsburg.

The locale for Stagecoach was to appear again and again in later John Wayne westerns. It was Monument Valley, Arizona.

When the Duke refused to continue to appear as Singin' Sandy Saunders because he could not sing, his studio Republic Pictures hired a new singing cowboy, Wayne's lifelong friend Gene Autry.

The Duke's first full-time job in films after withdrawing from USC was as a fourth assistant propman with a salary of $35.00 per week.

1. In The Comancheros John Wayne plays Big Jake Cutter. What type of lawman is Jake? He is a:

   a. Deputy Marshal.
   b. Town Sheriff.
   c. Texas Ranger.
   d. Civilian Scout.

2. Jake arrests Paul Regret (Stu Whitman) for what crime?

   a. for bank robbery
   b. for murder in Louisiana
   c. for cattle rustling in Texas
   d. for selling guns to the Indians

3. How does Regret escape from Big Jake?

   a. He rides off during an Indian attack.
   b. His girlfriend helps him.
   c. He hits Jake with a shovel.
   d. He bribes the jail guard.

4. Big Jake agrees to a dangerous assignment. He goes undercover as a:

   a. hired killer
   b. gun runner
   c. professional gambler
   d. prison escapee

5. Big Jake is forced to do business with the evil Tully Crow. The actor who played Crow was wonderfully wicked. Who played the part of Crow?

   a. Lee Van Cleef
   b. Lee Marvin
   c. Jack Elam
   d. Claude Akins

6. What is it about Crow that stands out most?

   a. The way he dressed.
   b. The way he drank and fought.
   c. The missing scalp from his head.
   d. The bowie knife that he carried.

7. Why does Big Jake have to shoot Crow?

   a. He catches him cheating at poker.
   b. Crow discovers that Jake is a lawman.
   c. Crow wants to kill an innocent man in a bar.
   d. Crow thinks that Jake and Regret are partners.

8. After Big Jake re-arrests Regret, what does he do to prevent him from escaping?

   a. ties him to his horse
   b. handcuffs him to an iron anvil
   c. makes him ride a small donkey

9. Big Jake and Regret don't get along
   until Regret does what?

   a. rides off during an Indian attack to
      get the Rangers
   b. helps deliver a baby boy for Jake's
      rancher friend
   c. saves Jake's life by shooting an
      Indian about to kill him
   d. kills a gunman about to shoot Jake

10. How do Jake and the Rangers repay
    the debt to Regret?

    a. They allow him to escape.
    b. They make him a Texas Ranger.
    c. They name a baby after him.

11. In The Comancheros, Wayne does not
    have the primary romantic lead role.
    This fact is important to the story
    since Regret's girlfriend turns out to
    be what?

    a. Jake's niece
    b. a crooked poker player
    c. the daughter of the Comancheros'
       leader
    d. the daughter of the Texas Ranger
       captain

12. Big Jake and Regret go to the
    Comanchero camp pretending to be
    gun-runners. What happens to them
    at first?

    a. They have dinner with the Indian
       chief.
    b. They are hung from poles to die.
    c. They are dragged behind horses.
    d. They are attacked on the trail by
       Indians.

13. The Ranger plan to locate the
    Comanchero hideout depends on a
    third Ranger who acts as the scout.
    This actor is killed and his body
    shown to Jake. Who played Tobe, the
    young Ranger killed by the
    Comancheros?

    a. Chris Mitchum
    b. Richard Jordan
    c. Pat Wayne
    d. Glen Corbett

14. Big Jake and Regret are finally saved
    from the Comancheros. How are they
    saved?

    a. The Rangers discover the camp and
       attack.
    b. Pilar, the leader's daughter, helps
       them get out of camp.
    c. Jake bribes one of the gang leaders
       for a wagon.

15. Paul Regret spoke like a gentleman.
    What expression did he use often that
    Big Jake didn't like?

    a. "My dear man."
    b. "My good man."
    c. "My friend."

NUMBER EIGHTEEN: THE WINGS OF EAGLES

1. The character who John Wayne plays in this film was a real life military figure. What branch of the service was Frank "Spig" Wead in?

   a. Army
   b. Navy
   c. Air Force
   d. Marines

2. What was Frank Wead's military specialty?

   a. He was a Naval sub commander.
   b. He was a Navy pilot.
   c. He was an Air Force Pilot.
   d. He was an Army tank commander.

3. What happens to end Spig Wead's military career early?

   a. World War II ends.
   b. He is court martialed.
   c. He falls down a flight of stairs and breaks his neck.

4. Spig amazes everyone around him by:

   a. remarrying his wife.
   b. learning to walk again.
   c. learning to write again.

5. While Spig Wead is in the hospital, he passes time by trying his hand at:

   a. designing a new type of transport ship.
   b. writing screen plays.
   c. designing a new type of airplane.

6. In the film, Spig is befriended by a movie director named John Dodge. Who is the real life director he is portraying?

   a. John Ford
   b. Frank Capra
   c. George Stevens

7. After his recovery, Spig pulls a lot of strings and gets back on active duty. What happens to end the second phase of his military career?

   a. His wife becomes sick and he gets a hardship discharge.
   b. He is seriously wounded during a Jap air attack.
   c. He suffers a heart attack aboard ship.

8. In real life, Spig Wead wrote the screenplay for a popular war film that starred John Wayne with John Ford directing. The film was:

   a. Flying Tigers
   b. Back to Bataan
   c. They Were Expendable
   d. Midway

9. The Wings of Eagles was a unique
film in the screen career of John
Wayne because:

a. John Ford directed him in color.
b. He had to age in the film.
c. He appeared without his toupee.
d. He appeared with Maureen
O'Hara.

10. The character of "Jughead" Carson
was pivotal to the success of Spig
Wead because:

a. He saved his life during an air
attack.
b. He forced him to learn to walk
again.
c. He shared his drinking habits.
d. He arranged for Wead's
reconciliation with his wife.

11. What actor played the role of Jughead
Carson in this film?

a. Dan Dailey
b. Ward Bond
c. Howard Keel
d. Donald O'Connor

12. What was Spig Wead's military rank
at the time of his accident?

a. He was a Captain.
b. He was a Commodore.
c. He was a Lieut. Commander.
d. He was an Admiral.

13. One of the early tragedies in Spig
Wead's life was the death of his only
son. What did Spig call his infant
son?

a. He called him the admiral.
b. He called him the commodore.
c. He called him the skipper.

14. In a bit of real life Hollywood history,
what famous leading man had a bit
role in Spig's first film Hell Divers?

a. Wallace Beery
b. Gary Cooper
c. Clark Gable

15. Spig is about to reconcile with his
wife and send for her to live with him
when what happens?

a. The Japs bomb Pearl Harbor.
b. He becomes crippled.
c. She dies of a heart attack.

NUMBER NINETEEN: REAP THE WILD WIND

1. In this film what was Captain Jack Stuart's (Wayne) occupation?

   a. He is an Army Officer.
   b. He is a merchant ship captain.
   c. He is a naval officer.
   d. He is a Marine officer.

2. The Duke actually played the second male lead in Reap The Wild Wind. Name the actor who played the romantic first lead. Hint: he was part of the famous British acting colony living in Hollywood during the 1930's and 1940's.

   a. Errol Flynn
   b. Ronald Coleman
   c. Ray Milland
   d. George Sanders

3. Reap The Wild Wind was a notable movie in The Duke's film career since it teamed him with one of the screen's greatest directors. The director was:

   a. John Ford
   b. Frank Capra
   c. Cecil B. DeMille
   d. Raoul Walsh

4. In what location of the United States is Reap The Wild Wind set?

   a. New England
   b. Florida
   c. California
   d. Alaska

5. The woman who Jack Stuart loves in the film was a popular actress of the time. She was:

   a. Susan Hayward
   b. Joan Crawford
   c. Paulette Goddard
   d. Claudette Colbert

6. Jack Stuart has a series of bad breaks throughout the film. What happens to him at the start of the film?

   a. He is knocked unconscious and kidnapped.
   b. He is knocked unconscious and his ship sunk.
   c. His command and ship is taken away from him.

7. Jack Stuart's rival for his sweetheart is the lawyer for the shipline he works for. When he thinks that Loxi is leaving him for Tolliver, what does he do?

   a. He pays some men to shanghai him.
   b. He runs his ship into a reef.
   c. He shoots him in a pistol duel.
   d. He lets him drown in a shipwreck.

8. The villian in Reap The Wild Wind was a well known character actor. He lied to Jack Stuart about Loxi's feelings for Tolliver. The actor in the role of King Cutler was:

   a. Charles Coburn
   b. Raymond Massey
   c. Robert Preston
   d. George Raft

9. Loxi's cousin in the film, Drusilla Alston, meets a tragic end due to Stuart's bad judgment. What happens to her?

   a. She falls from a horse and breaks her neck.
   b. She dies in child birth.
   c. She drowns while hiding aboard Stuart's ship.
   d. She is accidentally killed during a duel.

10. Jack Stuart redeems himself at the end of Reap The Wild Wind and proves that he was not a villain. What does he do?

   a. He saves Tolliver from being shanghaied.
   b. He saves Tolliver from a giant squid and drowns.
   c. He gives testimony in court against King Cutler and the shipwreckers.
   d. He helps Tolliver win control of the shipping company.

NUMBER TWENTY: THE LONG VOYAGE HOME

1. The movie The Long Voyage Home was based on stage plays by what American playwright?

   a. F. Scott Fitzgerald
   b. Tennessee Williams
   c. George Bernard Shaw
   d. Eugene O'Neill

2. This film is the Duke's first with director John Ford after the hit Stagecoach. What other member of the Stagecoach cast is in this film?

   a. Barry Fitzgerald
   b. Thomas Mitchell
   c. Andy Devine
   d. Ward Bond

3. What is unique about Wayne's performance in The Long Voyage Home?

   a. He dies in the film.
   b. He does not have the leading role.
   c. He speaks with an accent.
   d. He co-produced the film.

4. What is John Wayne's nationality in this film?

   a. German
   b. Irish
   c. French
   d. Swedish

5. What type of role is Wayne playing in this film?

   a. a member of the Coast Guard
   b. a merchant sailor during World War II
   c. a young naval officer
   d. a test pilot

6. Wayne's character Ole Olson has several narrow escapes. Which one does not happen to him?

   a. He is drugged and nearly shanghaied.
   b. He is injured in a bar fight.
   c. The ship he is rescued from is torpedoed.
   d. He is put on his ship to Sweden.

7. One of John Wayne's great off-screen friends has a memorable death scene in the film. Who is this actor?

   a. Victor McLaglen
   b. Barry Fitzgerald
   c. Ward Bond
   d. Grant Withers

8. What does Ole Olson carry with him when he leaves the ship?

   a. his mother's picture and letters
   b. his pet parrot in a cage
   c. his father's bible
   d. a tin box filled with his girlfriend's letters

9. How do Ole's friends realize that he has been kidnapped?

   a. The barking dog leads to his kidnappers.
   b. The talking parrot lets his ship-mates know that he was kidnapped, and not on the ship home.
   c. The black cat left in the bar is a give-away that he was kidnapped.

10. What was Ole drinking when they drugged him?

   a. beer
   b. ginger beer
   c. scotch
   d. Irish whiskey

CHAPTER FOUR

THE DUKE ON FILM: THE SELECT JOHN WAYNE

This group of John Wayne films represents a mixed bag of fine acting performances and Duke action films in which the action, rather than the acting, dominates the film. Remember, any John Wayne film is worth watching. So look in your local newspaper and cable television guide since many of these films appear regularly on television screens in most parts of the country.

RANK	MOVIE TITLE	YEAR MADE
21	The High and the Mighty	1954
22	Tall in the Saddle	1944
23	Flying Tigers	1942
24	Back to Bataan	1945
25	Hondo	1953
26	The Sons of Katie Elder	1965
27	Dark Command	1940
28	Operation Pacific	1951
29	The Fighting Seabees	1944
30	The Alamo	1960
31	Angel and the Badman	1947
32	Rooster Cogburn	1975
33	McLintock	1963
34	Big Jake	1971
35	The Green Berets	1968
36	In Harm's Way	1965
37	Wake of the Red Witch	1948
38	The Train Robbers	1973
39	The War Wagon	1967
40	The Cowboys	1972
41	Flame of the Barbary Coast	1944
42	Trouble Along the Way	1953
43	Donovan's Reef	1963
44	Flying Leathernecks	1951
45	Island in the Sky	1953

NUMBER TWENTY ONE: THE HIGH AND THE MIGHTY

1. The High and the Mighty is what type of standard formula Hollywood film?

    a. the sea disaster and rescue film
    b. the lost patrol and rescue film
    c. the airplane disaster and rescue film
    d. the corrupt politican's downfall film

2. John Wayne as Dan Roman plays the part of what?

    a. a Coast Guard captain
    b. an airplane co-pilot
    c. a merchant sea captain
    d. a construction company owner

3. Dan Roman walked with a limp. Why?

    a. He was born with a clubfoot.
    b. He was injured in the war.
    c. He was injured in a plane crash.
    d. He was injured in a car crash.

4. Dan is known to his friends by a nickname. What is his nickname?

    a. Big Dan
    b. Whistling Dan Roman
    c. Fast Dan Roman
    d. The Grey Fox

5. Dan is only a co-pilot but he is the real hero of the film. Why?

    a. He disarms a passenger with a loaded gun.
    b. He forces the pilot not to ditch the plane.
    c. He lands the plane safely in the ocean.
    d. He lightens the plane to save fuel consumption.

6. The male cast in this film was loaded with old John Wayne film regulars. All but one of the actors below have appeared with Wayne in two or more films. Which actor only appeared once with Wayne?

    a. John Qualen
    b. Paul Fix
    c. Paul Kelly
    d. Phil Harris

7. The female passengers were also stars from previous John Wayne films. Name the one actress who had not appeared with Wayne before this film.

    a. Laraine Day
    b. Claire Trevor
    c. Julie Bishop
    d. Jan Sterling

8. Who was originally to star as Dan Roman?

    a. Glenn Ford
    b. Spencer Tracy
    c. James Stewart
    d. Robert Mitchum

9. When Dan slowly walks away at the end of the film, what song is he whistling?

    a. Wild Blue Yonder
    b. Blue Moon
    c. The High and the Mighty

1. Rocklin (Wayne) plays poker and wins the last hand but is denied his money. What does he do?

   a. punches out the other card player
   b. goes upstairs to get his gun
   c. out-draws the other card player
   d. goes to the bar for a shot of whiskey

2. What hand did Rocklin win with?

   a. Full House—Queens over
   b. Two Pairs—Aces over eights
   c. Two Pairs—Kings up
   d. Three Aces

3. Rocklin meets Arly Harolday, played by Ella Raines, in the street. Rather than love-at-first-sight, she threatens to kill him. How many shots does she fire at The Duke?

   a. 2
   b. 3
   c. 4
   d. 5

4. Arly follows Rocklin to the line cabin on her ranch. They quarrel and she throws a knife at him. What does he do?

   a. slaps her in the face
   b. grabs her and tenderly kisses her
   c. puts her over his knee and spanks her
   d. throws a bucket of water at her

5. Arly fires Rocklin and he returns to town. What does he take with him into his hotel room?

   a. the young girl who has a crush on him
   b. his saddle
   c. Gabby Hayes

6. Rocklin is determined to find the killer of Red Kardell. What evidence does he find?

   a. a tobacco pouch
   b. a throwing knife
   c. a deck of marked playing cards
   d. a written letter of confession

7. What is Rocklin's relationship to Red Kardell?

   a. son
   b. nephew
   c. grandson
   d. cousin

8. What character actor and friend of the Duke played the villain, Judge Garvey?

   a. Ward Bond
   b. Gabby Hayes
   c. Harry Carey
   d. Paul Fix

9. The comic relief in the film is supplied by an old hand at being the hero's partner. Who is the actor?

   a. Walter Brennan
   b. Raymond Hatton
   c. George Gabby Hayes
   d. Andy Devine

10. The villain who tried to kill Rocklin in the line cabin ran off but dropped what outside in the woods?

   a. He dropped his hat.
   b. He dropped his leather tobacco pouch.
   c. He dropped his knife.
   d. He dropped his leather wallet.

NUMBER TWENTY THREE: FLYING TIGERS

1. What is Jim Gordan (Wayne) searching for in the early scenes of this movie while in Rangoon?

   a. supplies for an orphanage
   b. the enemy bridge to bomb
   c. more pilots for his squadron
   d. a Chinese restaurant for his date

2. What does Jim's love interest, Brooke, do in the film?

   a. She is the local doctor.
   b. She is the nurse for the squadron.
   c. She is the local school teacher.
   d. She runs the local orphanage.

3. Wayne has to make a difficult decision to replace and ground his second-in-command. Why?

   a. He has a drinking problem.
   b. His eyesight was failing.
   c. He accidentally shot down one of his own pilots.
   d. He disobeyed orders and destroyed a plane.

4. Among the new pilots is an old friend, Woody Jason, a good pilot but an arrogant loudmouth, who the squadron soon learns to hate. The actor playing this role never went far in his career. He was:

   a. John Lund
   b. John Carroll
   c. Gordon Jones
   d. Tom Drake

5. How much bonus money did Jim and his fellow pilots receive for every Jap plane shot down?

   a. $600
   b. $400
   c. $500

6. Where is Jim Gordon's hometown in the USA?

   a. Chicago
   b. San Francisco
   d. Dallas
   d. Boston

7. What does Jim's friend Woody call him?

   a. Pappy
   b. Tiger
   c. Bossman
   d. Skipper

8. Wayne's love interest is an English actress who never really achieved stardom. Her name is:

   a. Patricia Morrison
   b. Anna Lee
   c. Betty Field
   d. Binnie Barnes

The Duke was the first major star to produce his own films.

The first film in which the Duke died was in the 1942 film Reap The Wild Wind. His first death in Hollywood combat was in the 1944 film The Fighting Seabees.

The State Department asked the Duke to make the film Back to Bataan, a tribute to the guerrilla fighters in the Philippines. The film was released in 1945.

The Marine Corps in 1949 was suffering from a lack of enlistments. They asked the Duke to do a film about Marines. Wayne made Sands of Iwo Jima and enlistments increased by the thousands.

It was said that The Duke disliked Columbia Pictures mogul Harry Cohn so much he refused the lead in the western classic The Gunfighter. Gregory Peck starred as John Ringo in this 1950 film.

The Duke was very loyal to the media that supported him and avoided television in the early years. However, he did do some radio work in the early 1940's. He produced and starred in a radio series called Three Sheets to the Wind in which he played an alcoholic detective.

The Duke as the tough marine sergeant John M. Stryker from Sands of Iwo Jima which earned Wayne his first Oscar nomination in 1949.

9. Each of the aircraft in the Flying Tiger squadron had a number painted on its side. What was the Duke's plane's number?

a. 72
b. 70
c. 69
d. 41

10. In a break from the war, Jim takes Brooke to a Chinese restaurant for dinner. While there an old Chinaman plays the same record over and over again. What was the name of the song?

a. Blue Moon
b. As Time Goes By
c. That Old Feeling
d. Moonlight Serenade

11. What is special about this film in The Duke's movie career?

a. This was John Wayne's first war film.
b. This was the first film that Wayne died in.
c. This was the first film that Wayne didn't get the girl in the end.
d. This was Wayne's first technicolor film.

NUMBER TWENTY FOUR: BACK TO BATAAN

1. In this film the Duke is fighting in the Philippines. What branch of the armed forces is he with?

a. Army
b. Navy
c. Air Force
d. Marines

2. After the fall of Bataan what is he ordered to do?

a. Return to USA to train men for combat
b. form a guerrilla force to continue to fight the Japanese.
c. accompany Gen. MacArthur to Australia

3. Col. Joe Madden (Wayne) and his small band of fighters take a desperate risk to free Capt. Andres Bonifacio from a Japanese death march. Why?

a. He is a traitor who must be killed.
b. He is a close personal friend of Madden's
c. He is the son of a well known Philippino leader.
d. He knows where a fortune in gold is hidden.

4. What is the name of the well known actor who played the role of Bonifacio?

a. Cornel Wilde
b. Anthony Quinn
c. Richard Conte
d. Richard Basehart

5. Bonifacio, once freed from the Japs, is still depressed. What is really bothering him?

   a. He thinks his sweetheart has become a traitor.
   b. His family is in a Japanese concentration camp.
   c. He is angry that his country has lost the war.

6. A small schoolboy, loyal to the American and Philippino forces, is caught and tortured by the Japs. How do they know he is friends with the guerrillas?

   a. A Jap soldier finds a pack of American cigarettes on him.
   b. A Jap soldier finds a bottle of coke on him.
   c. A Jap soldier finds the Duke's Army colonel insignia on him.
   d. A Jap soldier finds an American baseball cap on him.

7. The Duke and his troops attack a major Japanese military base. How do they hide from the Japs?

   a. They hide in the surrounding jungle.
   b. They hide underwater breathing through reeds.
   c. They hide in boats along the waterway.

8. The Duke reports in by radio, and is ordered to headquarters. What does he jokingly ask for?

   a. A razor.
   b. More Japs.
   c. Some American cigarettes.
   d. Some coke.

9. How do the guerrillas signal the American submarine?

   a. They light bonfires.
   b. They wait in a boat flying an American Flag.
   c. They signal by wireless radio from the trees.

10. What major World War Two battle is the Duke providing support for in this film?

    a. The battle for Manila.
    b. The battle for Bataan.
    c. The battle for Leyte.

11. What is special about the ending of this Wayne war film?

    a. It has a request to buy war bonds.
    b. It has actual POWs from the Philippines.
    c. The Duke dies a hero's death.

1. When the Duke as Hondo Lane first walks across the screen, he is accompanied by a large brown dog. What is the dog's name?

    a. Lucky
    b. Sam
    c. Old Yellar

2. Which one of the following items is Hondo *not* carrying?

    a. a rifle
    b. a saddle
    c. saddle bags

3. What is Hondo Lane's current occupation?

    a. gunfighter
    b. lawman
    c. civilian scout
    d. bounty hunter

4. How did Hondo train his dog to smell Indians?

    a. He bought him from an Indian as a pup.
    b. He paid an Indian to beat him with a stick.
    c. He gave him meat whenever an Indian was near.

5. How does Hondo know that Mrs. Angie Lowe has been alone for some time?

    a. She tells him that her husband has deserted her.
    b. Her son tells him that his father has left.
    c. He notices that the ranch is run down.
    d. He heard about her at the fort.

6. In a twist of fate, Hondo has to kill Mrs. Lowe's husband. Why?

    a. They fight in a bar and he draws on Hondo.
    b. He thinks Hondo stole his horse and tries to ambush him.
    c. He accuses Hondo of cheating at poker.

7. Hondo removes something from the body of Mr. Lowe which saves his life when he is captured by the Apaches. What is the object that saves his life?

    a. Mr. Lowe's gold pocket watch
    b. a small picture of Mrs. Lowe
    c. a small picture of the Lowe boy

8. How do the Apaches test Hondo's courage?

    a. They tie him to a pole and throw spears at him.
    b. They tie him down and cut him with knives.
    c. They tie him down and put hot coals in his hand.
    d. They tie him over a camp fire.

9. Hondo survives being captured by the Apaches. What happens to his dog?

   a. The dog runs away to the fort for help.
   b. Mr. Lowe shoots the dog.
   c. The dog runs to the Lowe ranch for help.
   d. An Apache kills the dog with a lance.

10. Hondo has one last battle with the Apaches and his life is saved by a fellow scout named Lennie. What does Hondo give Lennie for saving his life?

    a. his horse
    b. his Winchester rifle
    c. his goldwatch
    d. his favorite handgun

11. When Hondo arrived at the ranch he helped the lonely lady and her son. What chore did he *not* do around the ranch?

    a. He cut some wood.
    b. He put horseshoes on the ranch horses.
    c. He sharpened an axe.
    d. He fed the goats.

12. What does Hondo tell Mrs. Lowe about himself?

    a. He tells her he is a former gunfighter.
    b. He tells her that he is part Indian.
    c. He tells her that he is a cavalry scout.
    d. He tells her that he killed her husband.

13. When Hondo goes to bed inside the ranchhouse what does he do?

    a. He places his dog along side him.
    b. He puts his rifle along side him.
    c. He puts his handgun in his hand and curls up.
    d. He uses his saddle as a pillow.

14. What is most important to Hondo?

    a. his word
    b. the truth
    c. winning
    d. destroying the Apache

15. How does Hondo confuse the Apaches in the final battle?

    a. He has the cavalry ambush them.
    b. He leaves the wagons in a circle to fight.
    c. He circles the wagons then drives off three times.
    d. He turns the wagons around and charges the Indians.

NUMBER TWENTY SIX: THE SONS OF KATIE ELDER

1. John Wayne plays John Elder the oldest of the Elder brothers. What is his occupation?

   a. Marshal
   b. gunfighter
   c. rancher
   d. Sheriff

2. Tom Elder was played by Dean Martin. He earns money by pretending to sell what part of his body?

   a. ear
   b. eye
   c. finger
   d. nose

3. All the Elder brothers except John attend their mother's funeral. What does John do?

   a. He visits the grave after everyone leaves.
   b. He has a tombstone made and sent to the graveyard.
   c. He watches the burial from atop a nearby hill.
   d. He sends a telegram to his brothers explaining his absence.

4. How is Mr. Elder, the father, killed?

   a. shot while getting off his horse
   b. shot during a card game
   c. shot during a gun duel
   d. killed by an Indian during a raid

5. Big John doesn't want to use his gun while in town. However, he does dispose of a paid gunfighter. How?

   a. hits him in the face with an ax handle
   b. breaks a chair over his back
   c. punches him through a bar room door

6. What crime are the Elder's framed for?

   a. stealing a herd of cattle
   b. killing the local sheriff
   c. stealing horses

7. How do they escape being framed and hung?

   a. Tom has a knife hidden in his boot.
   b. They dynamite the jail cell.
   c. They shoot their way out of an ambush.
   d. John's girlfriend brings him a gun.

8. Which one of the Sons of Katie Elder dies in the ambush?

   a. John Elder (John Wayne)
   b. Matt Elder (Earl Holliman)
   c. Tom Elder (Dean Martin)
   d. Bud Elder (Michael Anderson, Jr.)

9. When the Elder brothers are arrested and put in jail, what does one of them have with him?

   a. Tom Elder has a knife hidden in his boot.
   b. Matt Elder has a Bible on him.
   c. John Elder has a small pistol hidden in his boot.
   d. Bud Elder had nothing on him.

10. How does John kill the man responsible for his father's death?

    a. outdraws him in a gunfight
    b. shoots him with a shotgun
    c. shoots him with his Winchester
    d. shoots a barrel of gunpowder off

NUMBER TWENTY SEVEN: DARK COMMAND

1. Wayne as Bob Seton has a very unusual way of earning a living in the beginning of this film. What does he do?

   a. He sells phony medicine from a wagon.
   b. He punches men in the mouth to break their teeth.
   c. He sells phoney titles to gold mines.
   d. He sells guns to the Indians.

2. Who played the role of the dentist that Bob Seton works with?

   a. Walter Brennan
   b. Edmond O'Brien
   c. Gabby Hayes
   d. Frank Morgan

3. Where is Bob Seton from?

   a. California
   b. Kansas
   c. Texas
   d. Missouri

4. A famous cowboy star played a minor role in Dark Command. Who was he?

   a. Gene Autry
   b. Roy Rogers
   c. Rex Allan
   d. Tex Ritter

5. What Confederate soldier is Bob fighting against in the film?

   a. William Cantrell
   b. Jeb Stuart
   c. Stonewall Jackson
   d. Braxton Bragg

6. Bob Seton has a handicap. What is it?

   a. He can't talk.
   b. He can't write.
   c. He can't read.
   d. He can't dance.

7. Regardless of his handicap, Bob decides to run for what office?

a. town mayor
b. town sheriff
c. deputy marshal
d. town school teacher

8. Bob escapes a planned ambush, but just barely. How does he do it?

a. He falls off his horse and plays dead.
b. He sets his wagon on fire and hides below.
c. He drives his wagon off a cliff into the river below.

9. Bob shoots it out with Walter Pidgeon and survives with a little help from whom?

a. Pidgeon's wife
b. Pidgeon's mother
c. Pidgeon's brother-in-law
d. Pidgeon's sister-in-law

10. Who helps Bob escape from Cantrell's camp?

a. Fletch McCloud (Roy Rogers)
b. Mary McCloud (Claire Trevor)
c. Doc Grunch (Gabby Hayes)

NUMBER TWENTY EIGHT: OPERATION PACIFIC

1. Wayne is in the Navy again in this war film. What is he commanding?

a. a battleship
b. a P-T Boat
c. a submarine
d. an airplane

2. What is the name of his ship?

a. PT-109
b. Thunderfish
c. Tigershark
d. Nautilus

3. Wayne's character is called Duke Gifford. What tough decision does Duke have to make?

a. to ram the enemy cruiser
b. to surrender the ship
c. to avoid contact with the large Jap fleet
d. to take the ship down while the captain's on deck.

4. Pop Perry (Ward Bond) has a kid brother also in the Navy. What is he Duke's rival for?

a. command of the same ship
b. Duke's ex-wife
c. command of a special mission behind enemy lines
d. the naval cross for heroism

5. Who played the role of Duke's ex-wife in the film?

a. Maureen O'Hara
b. Vera Miles
c. Patricia Neal
d. Susan Hayward

6. Duke and his former wife meet again in Hawaii. What is she working as?

a. an Army nurse
b. a Red Cross Volunteer
c. a USO worker
d. a Navy nurse

7. Duke and his ship have bad luck in combat. What problem do they try to solve?

    a. improve the sonar equipment
    b. develop firing pins for torpedos that work
    c. develop ramming techniques for combat
    d. develop landing techniques for frogmen

8. Bob Perry still thinks that the Duke took the sub down too fast on his brother Pop. How are Duke and Bob reconciled?

    a. They fight in a bar, then make friends.
    b. Mary Stuart gets them together again.
    c. Bob is shot down and Duke rescues him.
    d. The sub crew tell Bob what really happened.

9. Duke thinks that his ex-wife's suitor is still a kid. How does he relay that message to her?

    a. He pats him on the top of his head.
    b. He saves his life.
    c. He beats him in a fist fight.
    d. He writes her a letter.

10. The Duke's love interest in Operation Pacific starred with him in another war film fourteen years later. In what later movie does she appear with Wayne?

    a. The Sea Chase
    b. The Wake of The Red Witch
    c. In Harm's Way
    d. Hellfighters

NUMBER TWENTY NINE: THE FIGHTING SEABEES

1. In The Fighting Seabees what did Wedge Donovan do in civilian life before joining up?

    a. He was a mining engineer.
    b. He ran an oil drilling company.
    c. He ran a construction company.
    d. He was a railroad engineer.

2. What did the Japs do to make Wedge mad enough to try to fight them against Navy orders?

    a. A sniper shot his girlfriend.
    b. A Jap plane shot three of his men.
    c. The Japs bombed the airstrip he is building.
    d. The Japs shot his best friend.

3. When Wedge finally joins the Navy, what rank is he given?

    a. Captain
    b. Lieutenant
    c. Lieutenant Commander
    d. Commander

4. The leading lady in this film appeared with Wayne two years earlier. What is her name?

    a. Donna Reed
    b. Susan Hayward
    c. Jean Arthur
    d. Claire Trevor

71

5. What happens to the Duke that is unusual in a John Wayne film?

   a. He dances the jitterbug and falls to the floor.
   b. He gets drunk and passes out at the bar.
   c. He plays the role of a coward in combat.

6. Wedge disobeys orders a second time and attacks the Japs. What made him angry enough to leave his position?

   a. the constant bombing by Jap planes
   b. the constant shelling by Jap ships
   c. the death of his oldest friend and teacher
   d. the death of his girlfriend

7. Dennis O'Keefe as Wayne's commander is wounded. He gives Wayne orders to hold at all costs. What does he also tell him?

   a. that he loves the same girl.
   b. that he is going to court martial him.
   c. that he is recommending Wedge be given command of the unit.

8. Wayne sees the situation getting worse. What is his plan to deal with the Jap invasion force?

   a. use tractors to push the Jap tanks off the cliffs
   b. catch the Japs in a murderous cross fire
   c. set an oil tank on fire to flood and burn the valley

9. What happens to Wayne during the final battle?

   a. He is ordered to retreat.
   b. His hand is burned from oil flames.
   c. He is killed by a sniper.

10. The Duke never really shows his true emotions to Susan Hayward until what happens?

   a. She tells him she is going to marry Dennis O'Keefe.
   b. She is shot by a Jap and nearly dies.
   c. He joins the Navy and she follows him.

NUMBER THIRTY: THE ALAMO

1. What American historical figure is John Wayne playing in The Alamo?

   a. Gen. Sam Houston
   b. Jim Bowie
   c. Davy Crockett
   d. Col. William Travis

2. How many men did Wayne bring with him to fight at The Alamo?

   a. 150
   b. 23
   c. 60

3. How did Wayne trick his men into fighting for Texas?

   a. He offered them land and gold.
   b. He suggested that they would be called cowards for not fighting.
   c. He faked a letter from Gen. Santa Ana promising to chastise them if they stayed and fought.

4. What does Wayne give the Alamo's commander as a gift?

   a. a bottle of Tennessee whiskey
   b. a wagon full of repeating rifles
   c. a pack of cigars

5. Wayne surprises the Alamo's commander with his knowledge of what?

   a. the Spanish language
   b. the political and military situation in Texas
   c. matters in Congress

6. How does Wayne die in the film?

   a. He is blown up by a cannon.
   b. He is stabbed in the chest with a lance.
   c. He is stabbed with a sword.
   d. He throws himself with a torch into gunpowder.

7. What historical figure did John Wayne originally intend to play when he planned making The Alamo?

   a. Gen. Sam Houston
   b. Col. James Bowie
   c. Col. William Travis
   d. Col. David Crockett

8. What fine character actor played the role of Sam Houston?

   a. Buddy Ebsen
   b. Richard Boone
   c. Lloyd Nolan
   d. Chill Wills

9. Who played the role of Smitty, one of Davy Crockett's men, who is sent with a message to Sam Houston?

   a. Fabian
   b. Paul Anka
   c. Frankie Avalon
   d. Ricky Nelson

10. The Alamo's meat supply of salt pork goes bad. How do Davy Crockett and Jim Bowie react to this problem?

   a. They take their men and ride away.
   b. They steal the Mexican's herd of long horn cattle.
   c. They get drunk and fight.

11. When Jim Bowie first meets Davy Crockett he calls him by a name that Crockett states he's trying to live down. What does Bowie call Davy?

   a. The Great Davy Crockett
   b. The Great Bear Killer
   c. Congressman Crockett

12. How does the Duke's son Pat Wayne die in this film?

   a. He is stabbed in the belly with a sword.
   b. He is stabbed in the chest by a lance.
   c. He is shot by a Mexican soldier.

NUMBER THIRTY ONE: ANGEL AND THE BADMAN

1. The film Angel and the Badman marked an important milestone in Wayne's career. Why?

    a. It was the first film that he directed.
    b. It was the first film that he produced.
    c. It was the first time he got top billing.
    d. He received a percentage of the gross.

2. When we first see Wayne as Quirt Evans he falls from his horse. What does he have tied to his right leg?

    a. a bowie knife
    b. a bandanna to stop the bleeding
    c. a Winchester rifle

3. We learn early in the film that Quirt Evans once worked for what western hero?

    a. Bat Masterson
    b. Wyatt Earp
    c. Wild Bill Hickok
    d. Buffalo Bill Cody

4. Quirt is seriously wounded but the doctor cannot get him to relax until:

    a. He hits him in the head with a pistol butt.
    b. He hands him his pistol to hold.
    c. He gives him a bottle of whiskey to drink.
    d. He has the farmer's daughter hold his hands.

5. What religious group does the farmer and his daughter belong to?

    a. They are Mormons.
    b. They are Catholics.
    c. They are Quakers.
    d. They are Jews.

6. The old Marshal, played by Harry Carey, is after Quirt. What is it he always wanted to do to Quirt?

    a. make him his deputy
    b. hang him with a new rope
    c. catch him in the act of a crime
    d. send him to territorial prison

7. Marshal McClintock is convinced Quirt is breaking the law. He watches his movements and in the end gets what?

    a. He gets to keep his six-shooter which falls from the wagon.
    b. He gets to keep his black horse.
    c. He gets to send him to prison.
    d. He gets to keep his prized Winchester.

8. Bruce Cabot leads the outlaw gang trying to kill Quirt. He almost succeeds. How does Quirt escape?

    a. A friend comes to his aid.
    b. The old Marshal rescues him.
    c. He hides under a waterfall.

9. Who does Quirt Evans send into the bar to challenge his three enemies to meet him in the street?

a. Quirt sends his girlfriend's kid brother.
b. Quirt sends the town telegraph operator.
c. He sends his blonde girlfriend.
d. He sends the town doctor.

10. In the final showdown, the three villains meet Quirt in the street. What happens?

a. He guns them down with his rifle.
b. The old Marshal kills the three of them.
c. He outdraws the three of them.

NUMBER THIRTY TWO: ROOSTER COGBURN

1. We learn in this film what Rooster's real first name is. What is his first name?

a. Horace
b. Marmaduke
c. Ruben
d. Clearance

2. Rooster is no longer a deputy Marshal when the film begins. Why was he retired?

a. He drank too much too often.
b. He got married and opened an eating place.
c. He killed too many criminals.
d. His past record caught up with him.

3. What specific crime did the outlaws he's after commit?

a. robbed a stagecoach
b. robbed a bank and killed the guards
c. killed an elderly Indian missionary
d. stole some explosives and killed the cavalry escort

4. Eula Goodnight is played by another Hollywood legend. Who played this part with the Duke?

a. Bette Davis
b. Katharine Hepburn
c. Lauren Bacall
d. Rita Hayward

5. Rooster and Eula don't like each other at first. He respects her a little more when he discovers what?

a. She is an excellent cook.
b. She in an expert horsewoman.
c. She is an expert shot with a rifle.
d. She also enjoys drinking.

6. Rooster and Eula have to travel downriver to avoid the outlaws chasing them. This led some critics to compare this film to another classic movie called:

a. The Sea Chase
b. The African Queen
c. Watch on the Rhine

7. In what western state was Rooster Cogburn a peace officer?

   a. Texas
   b. Arkansas
   c. Oklahoma
   d. Kansas

8. How long was Rooster a Deputy Marshal?

   a. 4 years
   b. 6 years
   c. 8 years

9. How many suspects did he shoot at the time of his retirement?

   a. 23
   b. 64
   c. 71

10. Where is Eula Goodnight from?

    a. England
    b. Boston
    c. Canada
    d. New York

11. What does Rooster call Eula?

    a. Old Maid
    b. Sister
    c. Old Lady

12. When Rooster and Eula go over the rapids on their raft, he promises what if they make it alive?

    a. to marry her
    b. to retire
    c. to give up drinking
    d. to go to church

NUMBER THIRTY THREE: McLINTOCK

1. The Duke is named after a President in this film. What is his full name?

   a. Andrew Jackson McLintock
   b. Thomas Jefferson McLintock
   c. George Washington McLintock
   d. Abraham Lincoln McLintock

2. What hasn't McLintock done in many years?

   a. He hasn't gotten drunk.
   b. He hasn't lost his temper.
   c. He hasn't played poker.
   d. He hasn't kissed another woman.

3. His wife Katherine returns home for what purpose?

   a. to take their daughter away
   b. to take over the ranch
   c. to finalize their divorce

4. When McLintock gets drunk what does he do with his hat?

   a. throws it in the air and shoots at it
   b. throws it atop the weather vane on his house
   c. throws his hat into the valley below
   d. he gives it to some Mexican children

76

In the 1940's the Duke became friends with Howard Hughes. Duke was under contract to RKO when Hughes bought the studio. Hughes produced three Wayne films which rank among his worst work. Flying Leathernecks and Jet Pilot were mediocre action films. But The Conqueror is considered by some as one of the worst films ever made. When Hughes sold RKO he bought the prints to The Conqueror and Jet Pilot for $12,000,000. Neither film was shown in public until after Hughes' death.

The sand used in the cement for imprinting John Wayne's footprints in front of Hollywood's Grauman's Chinese Theater was brought from Iwo Jima.

The Duke's best friend was actor Ward Bond. The Duke once accidently shot Bond in the back with a shotgun while hunting. When Bond died in 1960, he willed Duke the same shotgun.

The Duke and his best friend actor Ward Bond appeared in eighteen films together from 1929 to 1959.

The Duke's favorite sidekick in his westerns was veteran character actor George "Gabby" Hayes. He appeared with Wayne in fourteen films from 1933 to 1944.

Duke, America's favorite war hero, playing a Marine pilot in Flying Leathernecks.

5. How long has Mrs. McLintock been away from her husband?

   a. 2 years
   b. 3 years
   c. 4 years

6. What does McLintock play for relaxation when not drinking?

   a. poker
   b. chess
   c. checkers

7. How long has it been since GW McLintock has lost his temper?

   a. 20 years
   b. 30 years
   c. 40 years

8. How many times has McLintock thrown his cowboy hat on top of the ranch's weather vane without missing?

   a. 150 times
   b. 240 times
   c. 310 times

9. What does McLintock's old Indian enemy call him? The old chief calls him:

   a. Tall Shoulders
   b. Big George
   c. Big McLintock
   d. Brave One

10. McLintock gets drunk and tries to escort the ladies up a flight of steep stairs. How many times does he fall down?

    a. once
    b. twice
    c. three times

11. McLintock agrees to speak for the Indians at a government hearing. What tribe do the Indians belong to?

    a. Apache
    b. Comanche
    c. Cheyenne
    d. Cherokee

12. McLintock is the richest man in the state. What does he plan to do with his land?

    a. will it to his only daughter
    b. give it to the Indians for a reservation
    c. give it to the government for a park

NUMBER THIRTY FOUR: BIG JAKE

1. In Big Jake, John Wayne starts out searching for what?

   a. stolen money from his ranch
   b. his kidnapped grandson
   c. a herd of cattle stolen from his ranch

2. In the beginning of the film, what do several people think of Jacob McCandles?

   a. that he is the richest man in the state
   b. that he is the best shot in the state
   c. that he died

3. Early in the film, Big Jake prevents a group of cattlemen from doing what?

   a. stealing some of his cattle
   b. hanging a sheep herder
   c. shooting a group of Mexicans

5. Michael McCandles traveled with his father in an unusual way. How did he accompany him?

   a. He drove a model T Ford.
   b. He drove a motorcycle.
   c. He rode a mule.

7. Who played the villain that shot up Big Jake's ranch and stole his grandson?

   a. Lee Van Cleef
   b. Lee Marvin
   c. Richard Boone
   d. Richard Jordan

9. Besides his two sons and his favorite guns, what did Big Jake take with him?

   a. some dynamite
   b. his big black dog
   c. a model T car

11. What old friend of the Duke's played his old Indian guide in Big Jake?

   a. Bruce Cabot
   b. Harry Carey, Jr.
   c. Paul Fix

4. Big Jake was a real family affair. Which one of Wayne's real life sons was *not* in the film?

   a. John Ethan Wayne
   b. Michael Wayne
   c. Patrick Wayne

6. Big Jake carried a large trunk with him. What was in the trunk?

   a. his personal shotguns
   b. ransom money for his grandson
   c. cut-up newspaper

8. What did the villain say before he died?

   a. "You'll never get out of here alive."
   b. "I thought you were dead."
   c. "The game goes on and I'm winning."

10. Who played the role of Michael McCandles, the sharp-shooting son?

   a. Patrick Wayne
   b. Bobby Vinton
   c. Christopher Mitchum

NUMBER THIRTY FIVE: THE GREEN BERETS

1. What is the Duke's military rank in The Green Berets?

   a. Major
   b. Colonel
   c. General

2. What is his special mission in the film?

   a. to destroy an enemy bridge
   b. to set up special forces camps in the jungle
   c. to kidnap a Viet Cong general

3. Why does Wayne dislike George Beckworth, played by David Janssen?

   a. He is a Congressman opposed to the war.
   b. He is a newspaperman opposed to the war.
   c. He is a senior officer opposed to Wayne's plans.

4. Wayne accepts the torture of a Viet Cong soldier, why?

   a. He hates all Viet Cong.
   b. He leaves that decision to the Vietnamese.
   c. They found a lighter belonging to a dead Green Beret on the VC.

5. Wayne survives what near fatal catastrophe in the film?

   a. His helicopter is shot down.
   b. His jeep hits a land mine.
   c. His tent is hit by an enemy mortar round.

6. What member of the Star Trek crew is on board with The Duke in The Green Berets?

   a. Jack Soo
   b. George Takei
   c. Leonard Nimoy
   d. William Shatner

7. Who played the role of Sgt. Peterson, the company scrounger and reluctant warrior?

   a. Aldo Ray
   b. Bruce Cabot
   c. Jim Hutton
   d. Pat Wayne

8. The Duke is saved from what certain fate in this film?

   a. He is saved from a Viet Cong ambush.
   b. He is saved from a fatal booby trap.
   c. He is saved from marriage when his fiancee dies.
   d. He is assigned a desk job in Georgia.

NUMBER THIRTY SIX: IN HARM'S WAY

1. In this film, Wayne plays Rockwell Torrey. What happens to him during the attack on Pearl Harbor?

   a. His wife is killed by Japanese bombs.
   b. He loses his ship to enemy fire.
   c. He breaks his arm during a torpedeo attack.

2. What was the reason that Torrey's wife divorced him?

   a. He was having an affair with another woman.
   b. He would not give up his naval career.
   c. He did not want to have any children.

3. Wayne is promoted to Rear Admiral but has to deal with a senior incompetent Vice Admiral. The Fleet Admiral tells him to get the job done and refers to him as his:

   a. General Lee
   b. Stonewall Jackson
   c. General Grant

4. When Wayne meets his estranged son after many years, what does he want to do:

   a. have him transferred to his command
   b. throw him to the fishes
   c. join him on a double date with two nurses

5. Wayne's aide, played by Kirk Douglas, sacrifices his life flying over the Japanese fleet. The Duke doesn't think this act was motivated by heroism because?

   a. Douglas was drunk at the time.
   b. Douglas was guilty of raping a young nurse.
   c. Douglas was a coward.

6. Wayne falls in love with a navy nurse. What was her background?

   a. She was an Army brat.
   b. She was a Navy brat.
   c. She was a widow.

7. Wayne wins the final major sea battle against the Japanese fleet, but in the act loses what?

   a. His command ship is sunk.
   b. He has to have his leg amputated.
   c. His entire bridge crew is killed.

8. One of Wayne's junior officers in this film went on to star in a very popular television series. The actor was:

   a. Hugh O'Brien
   b. Michael Douglas
   c. Carroll O'Connor
   d. Stanley Holloway

9. What is The Duke's nickname in this film?

   a. He is called "Duke Torrey".
   b. He is called "the Rock".
   c. He is called "pappy".

10. Before Capt. Torrey was stationed at Pearl Harbor what military position did he hold?

    a. He taught at the Naval Academy.
    b. He was a submarine commander.
    c. He was commander of a destroyer.

NUMBER THIRTY SEVEN: WAKE OF THE RED WITCH

1. The Duke is known for his dramatic entrances in his films. In this film how does he first appear on the screen?

   a. steering his ship through a violent storm
   b. floating in the water tied to a raft
   c. pointing a rifle at the audience

2. The natives first thought Wayne was a god but later punish him by:

   a. making him dive for pearls
   b. throwing him to the sharks
   c. trying to burn him at the stake

3. How does Wayne get his revenge against the wealthy shipowner?

   a. He steals his bride and sails away.
   b. He steals his ship and sinks it.
   c. He burns down his plantation.

4. What is aboard the Red Witch?

   a. a fortune in pearls
   b. a fortune in diamonds
   c. a fortune in gold

5. What is different about this John Wayne film?

   a. Wayne did his own stunts while diving underwater.
   b. Wayne spoke with an accent in this film.
   c. Wayne drowns in the film.

6. The Duke falls deeply in love but is unable to marry his love because:

   a. He is married and his wife will not give him a divorce.
   b. His love is given in marriage to a wealthy man.
   c. He must marry the daughter of the island tribal chief.

7. When the naval authorities are after the Duke how does he escape?

   a. He blows up his ship and plays dead.
   b. He hides in the islands.
   c. He jumps ship and swims ashore.

8. How is the Duke saved from a fiery death at the hands of some native islanders?

   a. He is rescued by a group of British marines.
   b. A rainstorm extinguishes the fire.
   c. The Chief's daughter begs for his life.

9. Who played the Duke's beautiful French Woman?

   a. Joan Crawford
   b. Hedy Lamarr
   c. Gail Russell
   d. Paulette Goddard

10. What causes the Duke's death in this film?

   a. He is eaten by sharks.
   b. The Red Witch falls off a reef.
   c. Someone cuts the air line to his diving suit.
   d. He is killed by a giant octopus.

NUMBER THIRTY EIGHT: THE TRAIN ROBBERS

1. Where does the action begin in The Train Robbers?

   a. Mexico
   b. Texas
   c. Oklahoma

2. Lane (John Wayne) served in the Civil War with Rod Taylor and Ben Johnson and survived the battle of Vicksburg. Which side where these three friends fighting on?

   a. The Union Side
   b. The Confederate Side

3. In this film Ann-Margret played a widow named Mrs. Lowe. What did her husband do five years ago?

   a. He was killed in a whore house.
   b. He was killed in the Civil War.
   c. He stole gold from a train.

4. Lane agrees to help Mrs. Lowe. Before they ride off what is it he insists on doing?

   a. He wants to pick his own group of men.
   b. He wants to boil her shirt to shrink it.
   c. He wants to know the hiding place of the money.

5. Lane and his friends set out with Mrs. Lowe for where?

   a. Arizona
   b. New Mexico
   c. Mexico

6. Before Lane and the rest reach their destination, what happens to Mrs. Lowe?

   a. She is shot by a bandit.
   b. She nearly drowns while crossing a river.
   c. She falls in love with Lane.

7. Where is her husband's loot hidden?

   a. In an old Spanish church
   b. In an old gold mine shaft in the mountains
   c. In the fire box of an abandoned upside down railroad engine

8. When confronted with the large gang of outlaws, Lane puts Mrs. Lowe in plain sight of the gang. Who shoots at her?

   a. The outlaw leader
   b. The Pinkerton railroad agent
   c. The Mexican bandits

9. Who played the role of the mysterious gentleman following Lane and his men?

   a. Ed Asner
   b. Anthony Quinn
   c. Ricardo Montalban
   d. Ralph Meeker

10. Lane and his men refuse to take payment for their services. However, Lane rides off to rob a train when he learns what?

   a. The railroad will give a $50,000 reward.
   b. Matt Lowe was never married.
   c. Lilly from a house of ill-repute is on the train.

NUMBER THIRTY NINE: THE WAR WAGON

1. Wayne plays Taw Jackson who has just gotten out of prison when the film starts. How many years did Jackson (The Duke) spend in prison?

   a. one year
   b. two years
   c. three years

2. The Duke has no love for a hired gun named Lomax, played by Kirk Douglas. Why do these men dislike each other?

   a. Lomax stole Wayne's ranch and sent him to prison.
   b. Lomax shot Wayne but he lived.
   c. Lomax wants to steal Wayne's gold.

3. How does the Duke get Lomax to change sides and work for him?

   a. He offers him a $100,000 share in a gold robbery.
   b. He offers him a partnership in his gold mine.
   c. He offers him a bounty of $12,000.

4. Lomax is a man of many talents in this film. In addition to being good with a gun he is also:

   a. an expert with explosives
   b. a safe cracker
   c. an expert with horses

5. When The Duke meets the man who stole his ranch and had him sent to prison, he sees his personal property on one of his hired hands. What does the Duke take from him?

   a. The Duke takes back his gold watch.
   b. The Duke takes back his horse.
   c. The Duke takes back his hand gun.

6. The Duke takes a chance and breaks into his old ranch house. What is he really after at the ranch?

   a. a trunk filled with clothes in the attic
   b. the nitro hidden in the tackhouse safe
   c. his collection of shotguns

7. The Duke and Lomax nearly shoot it out in a saloon. What stops them from drawing?

   a. The local sheriff comes into the saloon.
   b. Some small Mexican children come into the saloon.
   c. The Duke's Indian friend starts a bar fight.

8. The Duke's plan to get his gold includes all but one of the following:

   a. blowing up a bridge to keep the rider's away from the war wagon.
   b. hiring the Indians to attack the war wagon
   c. blowing up the entrance to the gold mine
   d. hiding the gold in barrels of flour

9. What happens to the gold from the War Wagon?

   a. The robbers split it up and separate.
   b. The flour barrels overturn and starving Indians take the flour and gold.
   c. Lomax steals it all for himself.

10. Lomax is angry again with The Duke. What does he do?

    a. He shoots him again and rides off.
    b. He takes his share of the gold and rides off.
    c. He takes his horse and rides off.

NUMBER FORTY: THE COWBOYS

1. Will Andersen (Wayne) lost all his hired hands. Why?

   a. The Indians scared them away.
   b. Cattle rustlers shot most of them.
   c. A gold strike nearby lured them away.

2. Where does he go to find some new hands?

   a. the local prison
   b. the local school
   c. the local military fort

3. Wayne has to hire a cook for his cattle drive. What is unusual about Jebediah Nightlinger?

   a. He is a full blooded Indian prince.
   b. He is a former English nobleman.
   c. He is black.

4. Wayne's trail crew are followed by a gang of thieves. Wayne has a showdown with the leader, Long Hair. How does the Duke make out?

   a. He beats him bloody in a fist fight.
   b. He is tied to a tree and beaten by the gang.
   c. He bluffs him and forces him to back off.

5. What is so dramatic and unusual about this John Wayne film?

   a. the vulgar language and violence
   b. John Wayne played a man in his sixties
   c. The Duke is murdered in this film

6. Who played the role of the evil Long Hair?

   a. Dennis Hopper
   b. Bruce Dern
   c. Clu Gulager

7. In the film's end, what is it the cowboys are unable to locate?

   a. the original trail back to Will's ranch
   b. Will's actual grave on which to place his tombstone
   c. the hidden supplies left in the woods

8. What expression does The Duke use when getting the cowboys to take action?

   a. "Saddle-up!"
   b. "We're burning day light."
   c. "That'll be the day."

9. How many of the young cowboys die on the cattle drive?

   a. one
   b. two
   c. three

10. The Duke tells his trail cook what the members of his Civil War regiment used to call him. His name was:

    a. Old Lead Belly
    b. Old Hickory
    c. Old Iron Pants

11. The Duke eventually befriends all the young cowboys. He tells us how many sons he had that went bad and died. The number of sons The Duke had was:

    a. one
    b. two
    c. three

FORTY ONE: FLAME OF THE BARBARY COAST

1. What is Wayne's occupation in this film?

   a. a cattleman-turned-saloon owner
   b. a gunfighter-turned-saloon owner
   c. an ex-lawman-turned-cattlerancher
   d. a cattleman-turned-cardplayer

2. What state is Duke Fergus from in this film?

   a. Texas
   b. Colorado
   c. Montana
   d. Kansas

3. Duke falls in love with a singer at a casino in what big city?

   a. Chicago
   b. San Francisco
   c. Denver
   d. Dallas

4. Duke returns home, but cannot get Flaxen Tarry (Ann Dvorak) out of his mind. What must he learn before he can return to her?

   a. how to fast draw
   b. how to run a saloon
   c. how to cheat at poker
   d. how to operate a drug store

5. Duke returns to the Barbary Coast and succeeds in:

   a. getting elected to sheriff
   b. gunning down the card cheat who stole his money
   c. winning at poker then buying his own saloon
   d. buying back his cattle ranch

6. What does Duke name his new business?

   a. The Hen House
   b. The Silver Dollar
   c. The Golden Nugget

7. Duke never really feels comfortable in his new occupation. What happens to change his way of life?

   a. He loses all his money.
   b. There is a major earthquake.
   c. He falls in love with a school teacher.

NUMBER FORTY TWO: TROUBLE ALONG THE WAY

1. In Trouble Along The Way, John Wayne plays an out-of-work what?

   a. private detective
   b. basketball coach
   c. baseball coach
   d. football coach

2. The main female in Steve William's (Wayne) life is who?

   a. his wife
   b. his daughter
   c. his secretary
   d. his mother

3. Wayne as Steve Williams is a divorced man living with his small daughter. When he first meets the Probation Bureau inspector, he tells her his income is the same as a(n):

   a. banker
   b. investor
   c. tycoon

4. Wayne is offered a job that involves what?

   a. saving a Catholic college from closing
   b. creating a winning football team from scratch
   c. teaching in the classroom and coaching

5. When Wayne hears that one of his upcoming opponents is Notre Dame, he does what?

   a. He quits on the spot.
   b. He jumps up and cheers.
   c. He falls off his chair.

6. The Duke's daughter in this film was played by what young actress?

   a. Natalie Wood
   b. Sherry Jackson
   c. Sally Field

7. The Duke's daughter befriends Father Burke and gets him interested in what sport?

   a. football
   b. basketball
   c. baseball

8. By use of the movie flashback we learn why The Duke left his wife. She was:

   a. an alcoholic
   b. cheating on him
   c. beating their child

9. When things get tough, Wayne and his movie daughter talk about running away to an upstate New York city where The Duke has a friend who owns a bar and grill. What city do they consider moving to?

   a. Rochester
   b. Buffalo
   c. Syracuse

10. How does The Duke get the football players to play for his team?
    a. He gets them all scholarships.
    b. He gives them a percentage of the profits from each game.
    c. He pays them a cash bonus for each game won.

NUMBER FORTY THREE: DONOVAN'S REEF

1. Donovan's Reef is set on a Pacific island. How did Wayne and the rest of the crew get there?

   a. Their plane was shot down during WW II.
   b. They came on a merchant ship.
   c. Their destroyer was sunk off shore by the Japs.

2. What is Donovan's main business in the islands?

   a. He owns several saloons.
   b. He runs a small shipping business.
   c. He runs several clinics for the natives.

3. What do Donovan (Wayne) and Boats Gilhooley (Lee Marvin) have in common?

   a. They are cousins from Boston.
   b. They have the same war decorations.
   c. They share the same birthday.
   d. They love the same woman.

4. The name of one of Wayne's sailing ships is from an earlier Wayne movie. What is the name of the ship?

   a. Red Witch
   b. Wild Goose
   c. Innisfree
   d. Batjac

5. Donovan and Gilhooley have to signal Doc Dedham about his daughter. How do they do it?

   a. They use the native drums.
   b. They flash the light on the lighthouse.
   c. They use smoke signals.

6. The Duke greets Amelia Dedham (Elizabeth Allen) as she arrives by ship. What happens during their first meeting?

   a. She falls into the water.
   b. She slaps his face.
   c. She gets him arrested.

The Duke appeared in 21 films with his friend actor Paul Fix. Fix also wrote the screen play for one of Wayne's early western hits Tall in the Saddle.

The Duke wanted to attend the Naval Academy and loved the sea. It is interesting to note that most of his war films are naval stories set in the Pacific against the Japanese.

The Duke named his yacht The Wild Goose II after John Ford's ship The Wild Goose I.

John Wayne and John Ford made a total of eighteen films together, four before the Duke became known as John Wayne.

The Wayne and Ford combination used Monument Valley as the background for eight of their films together.

The Duke produced eleven films through his two companies Wayne-Fellows Productions and Batjac Productions.

The name of Duke's film company Batjac came from his film Wake of the Red Witch. In the film, Batjak was the name of his rival's shipping company. The name was misspelled during incorporation.

Duke ready for action against great odds in Rio Bravo, the 1959 minor classic.

7. Where is Amelia from in the States?

a. Chicago
b. Boston
c. New York

8. What secret is Donovan trying to keep from Amelia?

a. Her father is an alcoholic.
b. Her father is dying of cancer.
c. Her father married a native princess and has three mixed children.

9. Donovan has a friendly rival for Amelia's affection. Who played the role of DeLange?

a. Jack Warden
b. Cesar Romero
c. Dick Foran

10. The local French parish priest is best known for his role in what classic love story?

a. Gone With the Wind
b. Casablanca
c. An American In Paris

11. Amelia challenges Donovan to race her to the nearest shore. Who wins the swimming contest?

a. Donovan wins
b. Amelia wins

12. Throughout their courtship what expression do the two lovers use to resolve their minor differences?

a. "Let's be friends"
b. "Pax"
c. "That'll be the day"

NUMBER FORTY FOUR: FLYING LEATHERNECKS

1. The Duke is a marine pilot in this film. What is the mascot of his squadron?

a. fighting bulldog
b. the wildcats
c. the mustangs

2. What is Maj. Kirby's special theory of combat?

a. He believes in close air support for ground troops.
b. He believes in night combat missions.
c. He believes in precision daylight bombing.

3. The Duke's squadron gets its first assignment. Where are they sent?

a. Midway
b. Guadalcanal
c. Iwo Jima

4. What do they call the other leathernecks?

a. grunts
b. mud marines
c. dog faces

5. When one of his pilots disobeys orders and is killed, what does The Duke do?

    a. He writes to the pilot's family.
    b. He orders his men to look at the body.
    c. He requests more pilots and planes.

6. The Duke has one pilot in his command who is always out of uniform. What is wrong with his appearance?

    a. He always wears cowboy boots.
    b. He always wears a cowboy hat.
    c. He always wears a baseball cap.

7. The Duke is tough but in one scene regrets what action?

    a. He is sorry he court martialed a pilot.
    b. He is sorry he ordered a sick pilot to fly.
    c. He is sorry he punched his executive officer.

8. One of the Duke's pilots is an Indian who loses a leg. What tribe does he ask the Duke to write to?

    a. Apache
    b. Comanche
    c. Navajo

9. When the Duke gets leave and visits his wife and son, what gift does he give his small boy?

    a. He gives him a Jap helmet.
    b. He gives him a Jap sword.
    c. He gives him a Jap pistol.

10. How is the Duke wounded in this film?

    a. He is hit by machine gun fire while on the ground.
    b. He is shot down by two Jap planes.
    c. He crashes his plane into a Jap bomber.

NUMBER FORTY FIVE: ISLAND IN THE SKY

1. Wayne as Capt. Dooley is what type of pilot in this film?

    a. Army pilot
    b. Air Force pilot
    c. civilian pilot
    d. Navy pilot

2. What branch of the military does the Duke fly for?

    a. Army
    b. Air Force
    c. Civilian
    d. Navy

3. What happens to Dooley and his crew?

    a. They get captured by the Germans.
    b. They make a crash landing in frozen Labrador.
    c. They get captured by the Japanese.
    d. They crash land in the ocean.

4. What does Dooley threaten to do if any of his crew members tries to desert?

    a. He will have them court-martialed.
    b. He will leave them to the wolves.
    c. He will shoot them in the leg.

Film historians say that Stagecoach (1939) made John Wayne a star but Red River (1948) proved that he could act, and act without John Ford directing him.

The Duke's greatest personal undertaking as a movie producer was The Alamo. It was a personal project which he spent ten years developing. The Alamo was not a box office success although it did break even years after its initial release. The Alamo received twelve oscar nominations but won only one, the Oscar for Best Achievement in Sound.

The Duke was so popular that comic books were published based on three of his films, Hatari, The War Wagon, and The Wings of Eagles. In 1949, a series of comic books under the title "John Wayne Adventure Comics" began publication. The caption above his name read: "The Greatest Cowboy Star of Them All." In addition, the manufacturers of the detergent DRIFT published six Wayne comics as a promotion gimmick in 1950.

The movie Jet Pilot which The Duke made for Howard Hughes in 1950 was not released to the general public until 1957. Hughes kept adding footage but by the time the film was released it was outdated and failed at the box office.

The Duke played the same cavalry officer twice in two John Ford westerns. However, in the credits for each film the name is spelled differently even though it is the same character. In Fort Apache he played Captain Kirby York. While in Rio Grande, he played Lt. Colonel Kirby Yorke.

Duke in his favorite role as Sean Thornton in John Ford's classic film The Quiet Man.

CHAPTER FIVE

THE DUKE ON FILM: THE STANDARD JOHN WAYNE

This last group of films covers the full span of The Duke's long movie career. The fan will notice his aging as he continues to play the role of screen hero in a variety of parts. Hidden among the titles in this group are some fine screen performances as both the tough decent hero and the romantic leading man.

NUMBER ONE: ALLEGHENY UPRISING

1. In this early Wayne film, he plays Jim Smith an early American:

   a. marshal
   b. frontiersman
   c. Indian trader
   d. politician

2. In what part of the colonies is this movie set?

   a. Virginia
   b. Kentucky
   c. Pennsylvania
   d. Massachusetts

3. Wayne is fighting both Indians and who?

   a. the British
   b. dishonest traders
   c. the French

4. Janie McDougle was played by an actress who was to appear with Wayne four times in his career. The Duke's lady in the film was:

   a. Marlene Dietrich
   b. Martha Scott
   c. Claire Trevor
   d. Laraine Day

5. The second male lead was played by a suave British actor who would go on to win an academy award. Capt. Swanson was played by who?

   a. Ray Milland
   b. George Sanders
   c. Ronald Coleman
   d. Douglas Fairbanks, Jr.

6. The main villain was a character named Trader Callender. What popular character actor played this role?

   a. Brian Donlevy
   b. George Bancroft
   c. Thomas Mitchell
   d. Albert Dekker

NUMBER TWO: THE FIGHTING KENTUCKIAN

1. The Duke is in buckskins in this early film. As the title states, he is from Kentucky but where is the action taking place?

   a. Kentucky
   b. Virginia
   c. Alabama
   d. Tennessee

2. The Duke falls in love with a woman of European birth. What nationality is the Duke's girlfriend?

   a. She is Spanish.
   b. She is French.
   c. She is British.
   d. She is Portuguese.

3. The Duke goes to a fancy ball to see his girlfriend. He is mistaken for a member of the band. What instrument does he fake playing?

   a. The Duke fakes playing a banjo.
   b. The Duke fakes playing a guitar.
   c. The Duke fakes playing a violin.
   d. The Duke fakes playing a trumpet.

4. The Duke is captured in a bar fight and is about to be taken to jail. He gets out of going to jail by pretending to be what?

   a. The Duke pretends he is a doctor.
   b. The Duke pretends he is a dentist.
   c. The Duke pretends he is a lawyer.
   d. The Duke pretends he is a surveyor.

5. This film is noteworthy for the appearance of one half of a famous comedy team. Name the comedian who played the part of Duke's friend Willie Paine?

   a. Abbott or Costello
   b. Stan Laurel or Oliver Hardy
   c. Dean Martin or Jerry Lewis

6. The Duke dresses up to impress his girlfriend. What does he borrow from Willie Paine to complete his outfit?

   a. The Duke borrows Willie's coat.
   b. The Duke borrows Willie's Top hat.
   c. The Duke borrows Willie's pants.
   d. The Duke borrows Willie's pocket watch.

7. The Duke's girlfriend and her family are part of a group of exiles from Europe. Which country did they come from?

   a. Scotland
   b. Germany
   c. France
   d. Ireland

NUMBER THREE: IN OLD CALIFORNIA

1. In this western, the Duke did head west. What city did Tom Craig (Wayne) come from?

   a. Boston
   b. Chicago
   c. New York

2. What is the Duke's occupation in this film?

   a. He is a gold miner.
   b. He is a druggist.
   c. He is a physician.

3. The Duke has an unusual way of showing his strength in this film. What does he do?

   a. He picks up a horse.
   b. He bends a silver dollar with one hand.
   c. He overturns a supply wagon.

4. The Duke is nearly hanged in this film. What saves his life?

   a. His friends start a fire.
   b. The news of the gold strike at Sutters mill.
   c. His girl friend talks the mob out of hanging him.

5. The Duke is the hero in this film because he wants to do what to the gold miners?

   a. He wants to drive them out of the hills.
   b. He wants to sell them food and supplies.
   c. He wants to cure them of the epidemic.

NUMBER FOUR: DAKOTA

1. As the title suggests, the action takes place in the farm state of South Dakota. Where is the Duke from in this film?

   a. He is from California.
   b. He is from Chicago.
   c. He is from Boston.

2. The Duke was undercover in this film. Who did he work for?

   a. He was an agent for the railroad.
   b. He was an agent for the Confederacy.
   c. He was an agent for the Union.

3. The Duke is carrying $20,000 around with him to do what?

   a. He wants to buy a river boat.
   b. He wants to buy farm land for the railroad.
   c. He wants to buy cattle for the Union.

4. The Duke's lifelong friend Ward Bond plays a heavy in this film. What is different about him?

   a. He wore a full beard in the film.
   b. He shaved his head for the role.
   c. He walked with a cane.

5. The Duke saves the day and the
farmer's land. He wants to head for
California but what happens?

    a. His wife buys a large wheat farm
with their money.
    b. His wife buys a river boat with
their money.
    c. He is robbed of his $20,000 and
shot.

7. The film contains a solid performance
by an oscar winning character actor.
Who played the role of Captain
Bounce?

    a. Ward Bond
    b. Walter Brennan
    c. Grant Withers

6. The Duke's love interest in this minor
western eventually married the
studio boss. Her name was:

    a. Ona Munson
    b. Jean Arthur
    c. Vera Ralston

NUMBER FIVE: THE SPOILERS

1. The Duke played a tough hero as Roy
Glennister in this film. Where does
all the action take place?

    a. Texas
    b. Alaska
    c. Mexico

3. How do the Duke's enemies try to
eliminate him?

    a. They dynamite his mine.
    b. They accuse him of murder.
    c. They blow up his oil well.

5. The film's chief "spoiler" and the
Duke's arch enemy usually played the
good guy. His name is:

    a. Glenn Ford
    b. Randolph Scott
    c. William Holden

2. What is the Duke doing in this film
that makes him enemies?

    a. He is mining for gold.
    b. He is drilling for oil.
    c. He is mining for coal.

4. An old friend appears with the Duke
again in this film. What is the female
star's name?

    a. Gail Russell
    b. Claire Trevor
    c. Marlene Dietrich

NUMBER SIX: LADY FOR A NIGHT

1. Wayne as Jack Morgan plays a what in this movie?

   a. A New Orleans plantation owner
   b. A Mississippi gambler
   c. A steamboat captain

2. Most of the action in this film takes place where?

   a. in New Orleans
   b. aboard a river boat
   c. in Memphis

3. Wayne sticks by his former girl friend after she what?

   a. accuses him of murder
   b. is accused of murder
   c. cheats him out of his casino

4. This film is considered a lady's film with the Duke really playing second lead to the female star. Who starred in this film?

   a. Joan Crawford
   b. Joan Fontane
   c. Joan Blondell

5. The woman the Duke loves in this film owns what type of business?

   a. She owns a saloon.
   b. She owns a Mississippi gambling ship.
   c. She owns a hardware store.

NUMBER SEVEN: THE LADY FROM LOUISIANA

1. In this film, the Duke again plays a what?

   a. He is a sheriff.
   b. He is an attorney.
   c. He is a gambler.

2. Duke's co-star in this film was a European beauty. Her name was:

   a. Ona Munson
   b. Vera Ralston
   c. Marlene Dietrich

3. In what city does the action take place in this film?

   a. Atlanta
   b. New Orleans
   c. Charleston

4. The Duke again falls in love with a woman whose father is his:

   a. best friend
   b. boss
   c. arch enemy

NUMBER EIGHT: IN OLD OKLAHOMA
(also released as WAR OF THE WILDCATS)

1. In this action film, Wayne plays Dan Somers a recently discharged:

   a. criminal
   b. army veteran
   c. navy veteran

2. Wayne goes up against the local boss and they compete for the same woman and what else?

   a. water rights for cattle
   b. government oil land rights
   c. gold

3. The Duke visits Washington, D.C. and meets his old military commander who is now Commander-in-Chief. What President is portrayed in this film?

   a. Abe Lincoln
   b. Andrew Jackson
   c. Teddy Roosevelt

4. The President calls Wayne by his old military rank. What was he?

   a. a Lieutenant
   b. a Sergeant
   c. a Captain

5. The Duke falls in love with Martha Scott who plays a what?

   a. She is a librarian.
   b. She is a writer.
   c. She is a school teacher.

6. The Duke's first job after arriving in town is as:

   a. the town sheriff
   b. a body guard
   c. a stage coach driver

7. The Duke gets the rights to drill for oil on the Indian land and strikes oil. What stands in his way to fulfilling the terms of the government contract?

   a. His enemy has bought the oil pipe line.
   b. His oil wagons are burned.
   c. His well runs dry.

8. The Duke gets support in this film from an old friend. Who played the Duke's pal Desprit Dean?

   a. Paul Fix
   b. Walter Brennan
   c. Gabby Hayes

The Duke was often called "Big John Wayne." He made three films in which the title refers to his height. The films were: Tall in the Saddle, Big Jim McLain and Big Jake.

The Duke played six screen characters in which he had only one name. The names were: Rocklin in Tall in the Saddle, Ralls in Wake of the Red Witch; Wilder in Blood Alley; Temujin in The Conqueror; Lane in The Train Robbers, and Brannigan in the movie of the same name.

In The Duke's collection of films you will find twelve films with one-word titles: Salute, Conflict, Stagecoach, Pittsburgh, Tycoon, Hondo, Hatari, McLintock, Hellfighters, Chisum, MCQ, and Brannigan.

The Duke often said that The Searchers was one of his personal favorites. This appears to be true since he named his youngest son after the character he played in the film, Ethan Edwards. The Duke's youngest son is named John Ethan Wayne.

The Duke in his Oscar winning role of Rooster Cogburn from True Grit made in 1969.

NUMBER NINE: CHISUM

1. The Duke plays John Simpson Chisum in this film. Once again he is what?

   a. an aging lawman
   b. an aging gunfighter
   c. an aging cattle baron

2. Where is Chisum's ranch located?

   a. Texas
   b. New Mexico
   c. Oklahoma

3. What is Chisum fighting against?

   a. a government scheme to take over the mines
   b. the loss of his contract with the cavalry
   c. a crooked businessman trying to buy up Lincoln county
   d. a war with Mexican border bandits

4. What two historical western figures appear in the film?

   a. Jesse and Frank James
   b. Pat Garrett and Billy the Kid
   c. Wyatt Earp and Doc Holiday

5. Chisum lives alone at his ranch but there is soon a woman in his life. The woman named Sally is his:

   a. wife
   b. daughter
   c. niece

6. Chisum comes to the aid of an old Indian chief named White Buffalo. What tribe is this chief a prince in?

   a. Apache
   b. Comanche
   c. Cheyenne

7. The famous Billy the Kid is seen sitting by a river doing what?

   a. He is practicing his quick draw.
   b. He is fishing.
   c. He is reading the Bible.

8. Chisum fights the man trying to buy up Lincoln county by doing what?

   a. He visits the governor.
   b. He opens a bank and general store.
   c. He hires some extra gunfighters.

NUMBER TEN: CAHILL, U.S. MARSHAL

1. When we first meet J.D. Cahill he is going up against how many badmen?

   a. two
   b. three
   c. five
   d. six

2. As The Duke brings in his prisoners he sings to them what song?

   a. Swing Low Sweet Chariot
   b. Streets of Laredo
   c. Don't Fence Me In

3. In what state is J.D. Cahill a
   Marshal?

   a. Arkansas
   b. Oklahoma
   c. Texas

4. The Duke is wounded more than once
   in the same spot. Where is he
   wounded, and how many times?

   a. He is shot in the leg three times.
   b. He is stabbed in the left shoulder
      twice.
   c. He is wounded in the arm twice.

5. What does the Duke wear on his left
   wrist?

   a. He wears a long black glove.
   b. He wears a black wrist band.
   c. He wears a Comanche bracelet.

6. How do Cahill's two sons disappoint
   him?

   a. They both quit school.
   b. They get arrested for drunk and
      disorderly conduct.
   c. They help rob the local bank.

7. Cahill wants to teach his sons a
   lesson. He and Lightfoot try to scare
   them in the cemetery. What happens
   to Cahill?

   a. He breaks his leg.
   b. He falls off his horse who rides off.
   c. He is accidently shot by his
      youngest son.

8. How does Cahill track his sons?

   a. He hires Lightfoot to follow them.
   b. He rides after them at a distance.
   c. He walks after them until he buys
      a mule to ride.

9. Cahill uses the boys as bait for what?

   a. to locate the buried bank money
   b. to get the bank robbers out in
      the open
   c. to free the innocent men in jail

10. Who played the brief role of Denver,
    Cahill's ranch hand?

    a. Paul Fix
    b. Neville Brand
    c. Denver Pyle
    d. Jackie Coogan

NUMBER ELEVEN: EL DORADO

1. Wayne as Cole Thornton is a gun-fighter who rides what kind of stud horse?

   a. Palomino
   b. Appaloosa
   c. White Stallion

2. The local sheriff describes The Duke to a bartender how?

   a. "Tall man with an eyepatch"
   b. "a tall guy about six feet four"
   c. "an old guy with a Winchester"

3. The Duke and J. P. Harrah (Robert Mitchum) are friends from the good old days. What else do they have in common?

   a. They both love the same woman.
   b. Harrah has the same loop on his Winchester.
   c. They both wear two guns.

4. The Duke in self defense shoots a young rancher's son. He brings his body to his father. What is unusual about the way the Duke leaves?

   a. The Duke backs his horse up past the ranch hands.
   b. The Duke shoots his way out through the stable.
   c. The Duke is beaten and tied to his horse.

5. The Duke receives a near fatal rifle shot to what part of his body?

   a. He is shot in the right side of his back.
   b. He is shot in the left side of his back.
   c. He is shot in the back of the head.

6. Who shoots The Duke in this film from ambush?

   a. a hired gunfighter named McLeod
   b. the young rancher's son
   c. the young rancher's daughter

7. What is the Duke's horse's name in this film?

   a. Apache
   b. Cochise
   c. Bo
   d. Old Dollar

8. What happens to The Duke three times in this film?

   a. He is shot during a gunfight.
   b. He kills three men.
   c. His right hand goes numb.

9. Why does The Duke join forces with his friend Harrah?

   a. He is paid a $1,000 for the job.
   b. He feels he owes the rancher whose son he shot.
   c. He wants to prove he's better then McLeod.

10. The Duke has a young friend who is willing but cannot:

    a. ride a horse
    b. fight like a man
    c. shoot a gun

NUMBER TWELVE: THE UNDEFEATED

1. Wayne is once again cast as a what?

   a. a cattle baron
   b. a gunfighter
   c. an ex-Union colonel
   d. a lawman

2. What is it that Wayne wanted Ben Johnson (Short Grub) to do during their time in the Army?

   a. to salute him
   b. to call him colonel
   c. to stop eating so much

3. John Henry Thomas now a civilian agrees to sell his horse herd to the Mexicans. What does he meet along the way?

   a. a force of French troops
   b. the Confederate officer who fought against him
   c. a gang of Mexican horse thieves

4. Who played the role of the Confederate Colonel James Langdon?

   a. Lawrence Harvey
   b. Rod Taylor
   c. Rock Hudson

5. How do the two groups of ex-soldiers resolve their differences?

   a. They hold a boxing match between the two forces.
   b. They join forces against the Mexicans.
   c. Wayne leads the Yankees back to the states.

6. In this film, the Duke had two players from the same NFL team. Which two NFL stars listed below appeared with the Duke?

   a. Merlin Olson
   b. Jack Youngblood
   c. Roman Gabriel

NUMBER THIRTEEN: RIO LOBO

1. What was Wayne's last military assignment while on active duty?

   a. to escort a herd of horses for the cavalry
   b. guarding the Union army military payroll train
   c. escorting civilians to the stagecoach stop

2. As Cord McNally Wayne chases the Confederate troops who stole the Union payroll. What happens to him?

   a. He is shot in the leg.
   b. He is hit in the head and captured.
   c. He is stabbed in the shoulder.

3. The Civil War ends but Cord wants the Union traitor who gave the Rebs information on the payroll movements. Who does he ask to help him?

a. The Confederate officer who robbed the payroll.
b. The members of his old cavalry command
c. a Company of Texas Rangers

4. Wayne finds the traitor who now controls a small town. Wayne has to hold on to his prisoner and fight off the larger number of bad-guys. Sounds like what other movie the Duke made?

a. Red River
b. El Dorado
c. Rio Bravo
d. The Sons of Katie Elder

5. The Duke's friend shoots what well known non-actor in a barroom shoot out?

a. Joe Namath
b. George Plimpton
c. Glen Campbell

6. Rio Lobo was a disappointing film directed by an old friend who had made two other westerns with Wayne. The Director was:

a. John Ford
b. Andrew V. McLaglen
c. Howard Hawks

NUMBER FOURTEEN: BIG JIM McLAIN

1. In this film, the Duke calls upon the patriotism of what famous American?

a. Abraham Lincoln
b. George Washingon
c. Daniel Webster

2. The Duke is out of the saddle in this film and is playing what type of official?

a. He is a private investigator in San Francisco.
b. He is an investigator for the House Un-American Activities Committee.
c. He is a Federal Bureau of Investigation Agent.

3. What military branch did Big Jim serve in?

a. He was in the Navy.
b. He was in the Army.
c. He was in the Marines.

4. A blond landlady gives the Duke the nickname of "Old 76". What does it stand for?

a. It stands for 1776 and his patriotism.
b. It is the Duke's height in inches.
c. It was the Duke's room number.

5. Where does the action take place in this film?

a. San Francisco
b. Hawaii
c. Washington, D.C.

6. How did the Duke's partner die in this film?

a. He died of an overdose of truth serum.
b. He was stabbed in the back.
c. He was drowned.

7. How many communist agents is the Duke searching for?

a. five
b. ten
c. fifteen

8. The Duke falls in love with Nancy Olson and they relocate to his permanent duty station in what city?

a. Washington, D.C.
b. Los Angeles
c. Honolulu

NUMBER FIFTEEN: McQ

1. What type of character does the Duke play in McQ for the first time?

a. He plays a killer.
b. He plays a government agent.
c. He plays a police detective.

2. Where does McQ live?

a. He lives in a condo by the sea.
b. He lives on a boat.
c. He lives on a ranch in the valley.

3. Wayne drives a black Pontiac coup. What do they call his car?

a. Black Beauty
b. Smokey
c. Green Hornet

4. McQ is a divorced man with a daughter. What does he ask his ex-wife for?

a. He wants custody of their daughter.
b. He wants to borrow $5,000.
c. He wants to remarry her.

5. McQ is forced to quit the police force. Why?

a. He is suspected of drug dealing.
b. He is suspected of murder.
c. He beat up a local drug dealer.

6. McQ tries to get information from a middle-aged waitress named Myra. What does she call him?

a. A bear
b. a bastard
c. an S O B

7. What is McQ looking for in addition to the killers of his long time partner?

   a. the crooked cop in the force
   b. the two million in drugs
   c. the kid who stole his car

8. What is important about McQ's black sedan?

   a. It is crushed between two trucks.
   b. He carrys his extra guns in the trunk.
   c. The stolen drugs were hidden in the trunk.

9. McQ is without a license to carry his police gun. What does he get for an equalizer?

   a. He borrows a police dog.
   b. He borrows a rapid fire automatic rifle.
   c. He buys a pump shotgun.

10. In the end he discovers two sad truths about his partner. Which of the facts below are true:

   a. His partner was involved in drugs and murder.
   b. His captain was also involved in the drug theft.
   c. His partner's wife was involved and double crossed him.
   d. His partner was an innocent bystander.

NUMBER SIXTEEN: BRANNIGAN

1. Brannigan is a tough cop in what city?

   a. New York City
   b. San Francisco
   c. Chicago
   d. Boston

2. What is Brannigan's rank on the police force?

   a. He is a Captain.
   b. He is a Lieutenant.
   c. He is a Sergeant.

3. It is only said once it the film. What is Brannigan's first name?

   a. Mike
   b. Jim
   c. Joe

4. We learn that a top criminal has put a contract out for Brannigan's life. How much did he offer to kill the Duke?

   a. $5,000
   b. $10,000
   c. $15,000
   d. $25,000

5. Brannigan is put on a plane to bring back a criminal from what European city?

    a. Rome
    b. London
    c. Dublin
    d. Paris

6. Brannigan is a hard drinking cop. What is his usual drink?

    a. Scotch
    b. Bourbon
    c. Whiskey and Beer
    d. Gin and Tonic

7. The Duke is met at the airport by a policewoman. She makes reference to his height by saying that he was slightly smaller than the:

    a. Tower of London
    b. Statue of Liberty
    c. Washington Monument

8. We learn that Brannigan has a son. What is the son's occupation?

    a. He is a cop.
    b. He is a District Attorney.
    c. He is a stock broker.
    d. He is a doctor.

NUMBER SEVENTEEN: A LADY TAKES A CHANCE

1. This film was the Duke's first crack at light comedy. Where does the story begin?

    a. Boston
    b. New York
    c. Chicago

2. The female lead who played the "Lady" was a popular star of the 1940's. Her name was:

    a. Jean Arthur
    b. Martha Scott
    c. Claudette Colbert

3. How does the Duke meet the Lady in this film?

    a. He meets her in a saloon.
    b. He meets her at a bus station.
    c. He falls on top of her at a rodeo.

4. The Lady does something that nearly ends her relationship with the Duke. What does she do?

    a. She beats him at throwing dice.
    b. She steals his horse's blanket.
    c. She throws him out of her hotel room.

5. What does the Duke do to make a living in this film?

    a. He is a Marine pilot on leave.
    b. He is a newspaper reporter.
    c. He is a rodeo cowboy.

6. What is the name of the Duke's black horse?

    a. Sammy
    b. Blackie
    c. Bo

7. During the film, we learn that the Duke dislikes lamb chops, but likes to eat steak and drink what?

a. beer
b. tequila
c. Irish whisky

NUMBER EIGHTEEN: WITHOUT RESERVATIONS

1. This film is a change of pace for the Duke since it is a:

a. serious drama
b. light comedy
c. who-done-it mystery

2. Wayne plays Rusty Thomas, a Marine pilot, who falls in love aboard a train with a:

a. school teacher
b. librarian
c. writer
d. movie actress

3. The main plot of the film involves a trip to:

a. New York City
b. Hollywood
c. New Orleans

4. The film is also notable for the number of screen personalities that had cameo appearances. All but one did *not* appear in the film:

a. Cary Grant
b. Jack Benny
c. Louella Parsons
d. Gary Cooper

5. The Duke's love interest in this film was a popular leading lady of the 1940's. Her name is:

a. Loretta Young
b. Claudette Colbert
c. Donna Reed
d. Susan Hayward

6. The Duke's side-kick was a fellow Marine pilot in the film. This actor is noted for his comedy roles. His name was:

a. Jack Carson
b. Dennis O'Keefe
c. Don DeFore
d. Dan Dailey

The Duke used many names in his long film career. However, in Donovan's Reef, made in 1963, he used his own sons' names for the character he was playing. In the film he was Michael Patrick "Guns" Donovan.

In a 1953 change-of-pace film, entitled Trouble Along The Way, the Duke played a has-been football coach. This film was directed by Michael Curtiz of Casablanca fame and contains a famous line spoken by Wayne and later associated with football legend Vince Lombardi. The line the Duke spoke was: "Winning isn't everything, it's the only thing."

The year 1956 is significant in the Duke's career for several reasons. First, in the same twelve month span of time he made both his worst film, The Conqueror, and his best film, The Searchers. Perhaps he worked harder to make The Searchers a great film knowing how bad The Conqueror was. The other reason this year is significant is the Duke was exposed to a government nuclear testing site in Utah while filming The Conqueror. No one can prove that this was the source of his cancer in later years, but half of the cast and crew associated with the film died of cancer. Together, they represent a higher percentage of deaths from cancer than the national average.

Duke in his most controversial film The Green Berets in which he played Colonel Mike Kirby.

NUMBER NINETEEN: THE SHEPHERD OF THE HILLS

1. The Duke is really out of character when he plays a what in this early film?

   a. an illiterate southern farmer
   b. an Ozark mountaineer moonshiner
   c. a southern preacher

2. The Duke as Matt Matthews has to carry what stigma within his community?

   a. He killed his mother.
   b. He killed his father.
   c. He was illegitimate.

3. What was the Duke's mother's name in this film?

   a. Sarah
   b. Josie
   c. Mary Kate

4. What is the "curse" that the Duke was born with?

   a. He has a club foot.
   b. He has to kill the man who fathered him.
   c. He has a drinking problem.

5. The Duke gives his mountain girl a gift in the film. What does he give her?

   a. He gives her a lace collar.
   b. He gives her a small pony.
   c. He buys her a small cottage.

6. The ending of this film is rather dramatic and unusual for a John Wayne film. What happens to the Duke?

   a. The Duke shoots his father in a duel.
   b. The Duke is shot by his father.
   c. The Duke is shot by his girl friend.

7. This film was important in the Duke's film career because:

   a. It was his first starring role.
   b. It was the first film he produced.
   c. It was his first film in technicolor.

8. Who in this film is called "The Shepherd"?

   a. John Wayne
   b. Harry Carey, Sr.
   c. Ward Bond

NUMBER TWENTY: SEVEN SINNERS

1. The Duke is in uniform in this film and the son of a(n):

   a. General
   b. Captain
   c. Admiral

2. When the Duke becomes involved with Marlene Dietrich she asks for a penny for good luck. What does he give her?

   a. He gives her an English penny.
   b. He gives her an American Indian Head penny.
   c. He gives her a French franc.

3. It takes the Duke a while to get around to kissing Dietrich. What stops him the first time he tries?

   a. Her body guard won't let him near her.
   b. She is wearing an admiral's coat.
   c. She won't kiss on the first date.

4. The Duke's love interest is from France. What does Bijou do for a living?

   a. She owns the Seven Sinners cafe.
   b. She is a professional gambler.
   c. She is a cafe singer.

5. To symbolize that their love affair has ended Bijou (Dietrich) does what with the Duke's lucky coin?

   a. She gives it to a street beggar.
   b. She throws it into the ocean.
   c. She gives it to her maid.

NUMBER TWENTY ONE: REUNION IN FRANCE

1. In this early 1940's film, the Duke played Pat Talbot, a bomber pilot who is:

   a. on a secret mission behind enemy lines
   b. shot down in France
   c. a prisoner of the Nazis in France

2. To prevent the Nazis from discovering his identity, the Duke hides his military identification tag where?

   a. in the lining of his coat
   b. inside his hat band
   c. in the heel of his shoe

3. The Duke is saved when he meets an attractive lady in the street. They avoid suspicion by pretending to be:

   a. drunk
   b. lovers on the way home
   c. husband and wife

4. The woman who rescues the Duke from the Germans was the real lead in the film. The female star's name is:

   a. Hedy Lamarr
   b. Lana Turner
   c. Joan Crawford

5. The Duke punches a German officer while pretending to be what?

   a. A Swedish sailor
   b. An American student
   c. A Swiss businessman

6. The Duke falls in love with his lovely French lady and gives her what nickname?

   a. Angel
   b. Joan of Arc
   c. Mike

111

7. The Duke manages to get by the Nazis disguised as what?

   a. A German officer
   b. a chauffeur
   c. a French policeman

8. The Duke at first appears to be driving to Lisbon. What is his real destination?

   a. Casablanca
   b. Madrid
   c. London

NUMBER TWENTY TWO: A MAN BETRAYED

1. In this film, the Duke is out of the saddle and is playing what type of character?

   a. He is a policeman.
   b. He is a newspaper reporter.
   c. He is an attorney.

2. The Duke falls in love with a young lady whose father happens to be what?

   a. Her father is a local judge.
   b. Her father is a crooked politician.
   c. Her father is the chief of police.

3. Who co-starred with the Duke in this film?

   a. Gail Russell
   b. Loretta Young
   c. Frances Dee

4. The Duke spends part of the film investigating what?

   a. The suspicious death of his friend
   b. The local police force
   c. The local insurance company

NUMBER TWENTY THREE: THREE FACES WEST

1. In this early 1940 film, the Duke is not playing a cowboy but is a:

   a. farmer
   b. sheep herder
   c. moonshiner

2. The Duke wants to lead an entire town west. Where does he want to take them?

   a. California
   b. Oregon
   c. Texas

3. What is the problem that the Duke and his friends can't beat?

   a. The forest has burned down.
   b. The top soil is blowing away.
   c. The water supply has dried up.

4. The Duke falls in love but his girlfriend remains loyal to her boyfriend until what happens?

   a. The Duke proves that he is a coward.
   b. The boy friend is killed in Europe.
   c. The boy friend tells her he is a Nazi.

1. Where does John Wayne start out in this film?

   a. in the oil fields
   b. in the steel mills
   c. in the coal mines
   d. in the boxing ring

2. Wayne as a tough businessman makes then loses a fortune in what industry?

   a. oil
   b. coal
   c. steel

3. What really saves the character that Wayne is playing in this film?

   a. his love for Marlene Dietrich.
   b. his friendship with Randolph Scott
   c. America's entry into World War II
   d. his old boss straightens him out

4. In an unusual role, Wayne plays the what?

   a. dishonest cheat
   b. unfaithful husband
   c. cowardly liar
   d. alcoholic failure

5. The Duke first meets Dietrich on the way to:

   a. the union rally
   b. a boxing match
   c. attend mass

6. In one scene the Duke gets a suit on credit from a local tailor. The actor playing the tailor played a rare serious role without his usual sidekicks. His sidekicks were The Three Stooges, and his name was:

   a. Moe Howard
   b. Curly Howard
   c. Shemp Howard

7. In a fight between the Duke and Randolph Scott they battle around an open mine shaft. This fight was unusual for Wayne because:

   a. He accidently kills Scott.
   b. He loses the fight to Scott.
   c. He accidently injures his girlfriend.

NUMBER TWENTY FIVE: TYCOON

1. In this film, the Duke is a hard driving construction engineer working for a rich man in:

   a. Canada
   b. South America
   c. Mexico

2. The Duke tries to build a tunnel through a mountain but what keeps happening?

   a. He keeps running out of building materials.
   b. The tunnel roof keeps falling down.
   c. The men refuse to work in the tunnel.

3. The Duke takes the nice rich Catholic girl for a ride in his jeep and runs out of gas. They spend most of the night at an old Inca temple. What happens to the Duke?

   a. He has to marry the girl.
   b. He gets fired by the girl's father.
   c. He is shot by the girl's brother.

4. When the mountain beats the Duke and he stops work on the tunnel what does he do?

   a. He fires his construction boss.
   b. He dynamites the tunnel entrance.
   c. He quits his job and goes to work for another company.

5. When one of the Duke's men is dying in the tunnel he makes him promise to do what?

   a. He asks the Duke to bury him in the tunnel.
   b. He asks the Duke to build the bridge across the river.
   c. He tells the Duke to marry his rich girlfriend.

6. The actress who played the rich South American girl was once married to a famous baseball player and manager. Her name was:

   a. Claire Trevor
   b. Laraine Day
   c. Jean Arthur

7. By the end of the film, the Duke has built his bridge across the river and it survives what natural disaster?

   a. an earthquake
   b. a landslide
   c. a flash flood

114

NUMBER TWENTY SIX: CIRCUS WORLD

1. Wayne played Matt Masters the owner of a circus. He raised Toni Alfredo (Claudia Cardinale) like a daughter but kept what secret from her?

   a. He is her real father.
   b. He killed her father.
   c. He was her mother's secret lover.

2. What was Toni's mother in the circus?

   a. a bareback horse rider
   b. a high wire aerialist
   c. an animal trainer

3. Matt Masters has bad luck when he comes to Europe. Which event does not happen to his circus?

   a. His ship capsizes.
   b. His performers quit and join another circus.
   c. His big tent catches on fire.

4. Matt decides to return to his old circus act. What does he practice doing?

   a. driving a speeding stagecoach
   b. jumping into the saddle of a moving horse
   c. shooting balloons off a spinning wheel

5. The Duke's girlfriend disappeared after a fatal circus accident Where did she hide?

   a. She joined a convent.
   b. She fled to South America.
   c. She went in hiding in Europe.

6. Who played the role of the Duke's lost love?

   a. Lana Turner
   b. Rita Hayworth
   c. Betty Hutton

NUMBER TWENTY SEVEN: HELLFIGHTERS

1. The Duke in the role of Chance Buckman was actually playing real life hero Red Adair in this change of pace film. What does the Duke do for a living in this film?

   a. He is a test pilot.
   b. He is an oil well fire fighter.
   c. He is a war hero.

2. The indestructable Duke is seriously injured in the early minutes of this film. How is he hurt?

   a. He is seriously burned in a flash fire.
   b. He is shot by a rebel sniper.
   c. He is crushed by the blade of a tractor.

3. The Duke's New Year's Eve plans are changed when he agrees to take on an assignment in what country?

a. Mexico
b. Malaya
c. Malta

4. The Duke has to punch out some workers to get them to report on the job early and sober. What nationality are these workers?

a. Australians
b. Americans
c. Mexicans

5. The Duke's daughter in the film has not seen her father in how many years?

a. five years
b. ten years
c. fifteen years

6. The Duke comes out of retirement and accepts an assignment that takes him to what country?

a. Venezuela
b. Columbia
c. Peru

7. The Duke has to overcome guerrilla snipers to accomplish his greatest challenge. What must he do?

a. The Duke has to put out three oil well fires.
b. The Duke has to put out five oil well fires.
c. The Duke has to put out two oil well fires.

NUMBER TWENTY EIGHT: THE SEA CHASE

1. The Duke is at sea again in this film. Under what flag is he sailing?

a. American
b. British
c. German
d. Swedish

2. What is it he is trying to avoid throughout the film?

a. Japanese submarines
b. German naval forces
c. British naval forces
d. Russian naval forces

3. The Duke falls in love with a beautiful blond who turns out to be what?

a. the wife of his best friend
b. a German spy
c. a Russian spy
d. a jewel thief

4. The Duke is usually indestructable but in The Sea Chase the audience is left to guess what happens to him:

a. He and Elsa Keller sink with the ship and drown.
b. He and Elsa get into a life boat and find safety in Norway.

5. Who played the beautiful blond that the Duke falls in love with?

   a. Lana Turner
   b. Anita Ekberg
   c. Marlene Dietrich

6. One of the Duke's crewmen gets drunk and later realizes that he has a flag tattooed on his back. What flag is it?

   a. American Flag
   b. British Flag
   c. German Flag

NUMBER TWENTY NINE: LEGEND OF THE LOST

1. In what exotic city does Joe January earn his living in Legend of the Lost?

   a. The Duke is in Casablanca.
   b. The Duke is in Timbuktu.
   c. The Duke is in Cairo.

2. When we first see the Duke where is he living?

   a. He is living in a brothel.
   b. He is living in a saloon.
   c. He has moved into the local jail.

3. What does Joe January (Wayne) do for a living in Legend of the Lost?

   a. The Duke is a big game hunter.
   b. The Duke is an archaeologist.
   c. The Duke is a desert guide.

4. What type of animal does the Duke mount in this film?

   a. The Duke rides a camel.
   b. The Duke rides a mule.
   c. The Duke rides a horse.

5. The Duke's love interest in this film is a:

   a. professor's wife
   b. local prostitute
   c. nite club singer

6. The Duke and his friends find some lost treasure where?

   a. buried in a wall
   b. under a pillar
   c. buried in a bat cave

7. What is the name of the Duke's mule?

   a. Sophia
   b. Jenny
   c. Janet

8. The Duke and his girl nearly die in the desert. What saves their lives?

   a. The Duke finds water.
   b. The Duke finds a can of peaches.
   c. A camel caravan comes along.

9. The Duke almost dies in this film. How is he injured?

   a. The Duke is stabbed in the back.
   b. The Duke is shot in the back.
   c. The Duke is hit in the head.

NUMBER THIRTY: HATARI

1. As Sean Mercer, the Duke is not chasing cattle but what?

   a. renegade white hunters
   b. exotic wild animals for zoos
   c. roving bands of killer tribesmen

2. The Duke's love interest in this film is not accepted at first. What is her profession?

   a. She is a writer.
   b. She is a veterinarian.
   c. She is a photographer.

3. The sound track from this film contains a popular instrumental written by what popular Hollywood song writer?

   a. Johnny Mercer
   b. Henry Mancini
   c. Richard Rogers

4. Wayne falls in love with the outsider after she proves herself. Who played the role of Dallas?

   a. Sophia Loren
   b. Claudia Cardinale
   c. Elsa Martinelli

5. Where does the Duke ride when he's chasing wild animals?

   a. The Duke rides on the roof of a truck.
   b. The Duke rides on the left front fender of a truck.
   c. The Duke rides in the back of the truck.

6. What animal does the Duke have a problem catching?

   a. A Tiger
   b. An Elephant
   c. A Rhino

7. What does one of the Duke's driver's call him?

   a. "Boss man"
   b. "Bawana"
   c. "Big man"

8. How many baby elephants does the Duke's woman adopt?

   a. one
   b. two
   c. three

9. How does the Duke's girl let him know that she loves him?

   a. She gets into his bed.
   b. She asks him how he likes to kiss.
   c. She gets drunk and tells him.

NUMBER THIRTY ONE: BLOOD ALLEY

1. When this film begins, the Duke is in prison. Who are his captors?

   a. The Japanese
   b. The Chinese Communists
   c. The Russian Communists

2. The Duke escapes from prison by dressing as what?

   a. He dresses as a monk.
   b. He dresses as a peasant.
   c. He dresses as a Russian officer.

3. The Duke survived the two years in prison and the attempts at brain washing by what trick?

   a. He pretended to be crazy.
   b. He talked to an imaginary lady called "Baby".
   c. He pretended to believe their lies.

4. The entire village wants the Duke to do what?

   a. Teach them to defend themselves.
   b. Help them to steal a large tramp steamer.
   c. Take them to Hong Kong.

5. The villagers steal the local ferry boat. Where was the ferry boat built?

   a. Liverpool
   b. Sacramento
   c. Hong Kong

6. Blood Alley was a change of pace film for the Duke. Who was the actor originally signed to star in this film?

   a. Glenn Ford
   b. Spencer Tracy
   c. Robert Mitchum

NUMBER THIRTY TWO: JET PILOT

1. This film, although made in 1950, was not released to the general public until:

   a. 1952
   b. 1955
   c. 1957

2. Wayne played Col. Shannon an Air Force jet pilot who:

   a. breaks the sound barrier
   b. pretends to defect to the Russians
   c. is in combat in Korea against the Chinese

3. What do the Communists do to Wayne in this film?

   a. They give him a truth drug to get information.
   b. They torture him to get information.
   c. They give him a drug to erase his memory.

4. What does The Duke steal from the Commies?

   a. the secret plans for their radar
   b. a female Russian spy
   c. their latest rocket plane

5. The Duke's problems begin when he what?

   a. crashes a new fighter plane
   b. falls in love with a Soviet agent
   c. gets court martialed for insubordination

7. The role of the blond Russian pilot and secret agent was played by a young:

   a. Vera Miles
   b. Lana Turner
   c. Janet Leigh

6. The man who produced this film was himself a famous pilot. He was:

   a. Howard Hawks
   b. Howard Hughes
   c. John Ford

CHAPTER SIX

THE DUKE ON FILM: THE CAMEO ROLES

The Duke appeared in a half dozen cameo roles in his long film career. The cameo appearances range from a single spoken line in The Greatest Story Ever Told to a small but significant supporting role in The Longest Day. Regardless of the size of the role, the name John Wayne in the credits was certain to draw at the box office. Listed below are questions from The Duke's cameo appearances for your consideration.

1. In the Greatest Story Ever Told, The Duke played an unusual role and spoke one line as:

    a. the Good Samaritan
    b. a Roman Centurion
    c. a Roman Governor

2. In The Greatest Story Ever Told what Biblical event did The Duke witness?

    a. the birth of Christ
    b. the death of John the Baptist
    c. the death of Jesus Christ

3. In Cast A Giant Shadow, The Duke appeared opposite an actor he was to co-star with in two later films. The actor who had the lead in the film was:

    a. William Holden
    b. Frank Sinatra
    c. Kirk Douglas

4. In Cast A Giant Shadow, The Duke was in military uniform again. What rank was he in this film?

    a. Admiral
    b. General
    c. Colonel

5. What country does The Duke help in Cast A Giant Shadow?

    a. Greece
    b. Italy
    c. Israel

6. How does The Duke help his former military aide's country in Cast A Giant Shadow?

    a. He gets them arms and supplies.
    b. He helps the Jewish refugees into Palestine.
    c. He helps them get United Nations recognition.

7. In How The West Was Won, The Duke was directed in his sequence by what old friend?

    a. Howard Hawks
    b. John Ford
    c. Henry Hathaway

8. In How The West Was Won, The Duke had a beard and smoked a cigar as:

    a. General Ulysses S. Grant
    b. General George A. Custer
    c. General William T. Sherman

9. The actor who played opposite The Duke in How The West Was Won later starred in Wayne's last film with him. His name is:

   a. James Stewart
   b. Harry Morgan
   c. Gregory Peck

10. In I Married A Woman, The Duke appeared in his first cameo role married to who?

    a. Diana Dors
    b. Nancy Olson
    c. Angie Dickinson

11. The star of I Married A Woman was a popular comedian of the time. His name is:

    a. Bob Hope
    b. George Gobel
    c. Alan Young

12. In The Longest Day, The Duke's character in the film suffers some bad luck the first time in battle. What happens to him?

    a. He breaks his ankle.
    b. He lands behind German lines.
    c. He is shot in the arm.

13. In The Longest Day, The Duke tells his troops to use a five cent toy to identify themselves in combat. What kind of toy is he talking about?

    a. a small toy whistle
    b. a small toy mirror
    c. a small metal clicker

14. In The Longest Day, what branch of the military is The Duke in?

    a. Navy
    b. Army
    c. Air Force

15. In The Longest Day, how does The Duke lead his troops after his injury?

    a. He is driven in a jeep.
    b. He is pulled in a two wheeled wooden cart.
    c. He rides atop a tank.

CHAPTER SEVEN

THE DUKE ON FILM: THE WORST OF JOHN WAYNE FILMS

The Duke, himself, even admitted that he had made a few films that he was embarrassed to talk about. However, with the exception of one film that I will list below, this is a difficult category to write about since I believe that even a bad John Wayne movie is better than no John Wayne movie at all. So, I will identify the one film that everyone agrees was his worst and two other films that fell short of fan expectations.

THE WORST FILM: THE CONQUEROR – 1956 The Duke as the mongol chieftain Genghis Khan ??? Nothing more need be said about this classic instance of mis-casting.

ROLES THE DUKE SHOULD HAVE AVOIDED: THE BARBARIAN AND THE GEISHA – 1958 The Duke as the first consul-general to Japan. This film did so poorly it dropped the Duke from the Top Ten Motion Picture Herald's annual poll for the first time in ten years. He made it back in 1959.

THE GREATEST STORY EVER TOLD – 1965: Thank God this was only a brief cameo appearance as the Roman Centurion who witnessed the crucifixion of Jesus Christ.

NUMBER ONE: THE CONQUEROR

1. In an unusual role for The Duke he played what historical figure?

   a. El Cid
   b. William the Conqueror
   c. Genghis Khan
   d. Attila the Hun

2. What country is the Duke's character from?

   a. Turkey
   b. China
   c. India
   d. Mongolia

3. The Duke's love interest plays the role of a Princess. Who appeared with Wayne in this box office flop?

   a. Martha Hyer
   b. Debra Paget
   c. Susan Hayward
   d. Yvonne De Carlo

4. What studio head produced this film?

   a. Herbert Yates
   b. Howard Hughes
   c. Lewis B. Mayer
   d. Jack Warner

5. The Duke's blood tells him he must take the Tartar princess as his wife even though her father:

   a. poisoned the Duke's father
   b. leads the largest tribe in the Gobi Desert
   c. is ally with the Chinese warlords

6. The Duke survives a deadly attack by the Tartars. How?

   a. He hides in a cave.
   b. He hides under a bush.
   c. He rides off into the desert.

7. When the Tartars capture the Duke what does his wife make him do to punish him?

   a. He is given the slow death.
   b. He is made to pull her wagon with the oxen.
   c. He is staked out on the ground to die.

8. The Duke conquered all but at the movie's end he must do what?

   a. He must kill his best friend.
   b. He must put his mother to death.
   c. He must put his wife to death.

NUMBER TWO: THE BARBARIAN AND THE GEISHA

1. The Duke played an American historical figure named Townsend Harris who was:

   a. A New England whaling ship captain
   b. the first American Diplomat sent to Japan
   c. the first American to trade with China

2. A well known character actor played the role of Henry Heusken, the Duke's foreign language interpreter. His name is:

   a. Walter Brennan
   b. Sam Jaffe
   c. Paul Fix

3. In a dramatic scene the Duke prevents an American ship from being fired upon. How does he do it?

   a. He stands in front of the cannon.
   b. He waves the American Flag.
   c. He protests the action to the local governor.

4. The Duke overcomes a cholera epidemic by taking radical action. What does he do that gets him arrested?

   a. He forces the town people to be vaccinated.
   b. He burns down the village.
   c. He relocates the entire village.

5. Every John Wayne movie has its traditional fight scene and this one was no different. However, what happens to the Duke when he takes on two villains?

   a. He knocks them both out.
   b. He is beaten by the large man.
   c. He is beaten by the small man.

6. Who was the President that sent Townsend Harris on his mission?

   a. Abraham Lincoln
   b. Franklin Pierce
   c. James Monroe

CHAPTER EIGHT

THE DUKE TRIVIA ROUNDUP

JOHN WAYNE....the name brings forth distinct, strong images. The wrinkled brow when he is embarrassed or acting shy with the woman he's after...the smooth, rolling way he walked and rode a horse. The clenched jaws when angry and his soft short manner of speech. All of these mannerisms which have come to personify the Duke's screen character were perfected in the lean hungry years of B and C westerns. Of all the hundreds of would-be stars who labored in the mill of "B" films known by Hollywood historians as Poverty Row, only one actor survived the experience to become a major Grade A superstar. You guessed it, it was John Wayne.

NUMBER ONE: THE JOHN FORD CONNECTION

1. How many films did John Ford direct John Wayne in?

   a. 10
   b. 12
   c. 14
   d. 16

2. How many Westerns did Ford direct The Duke in over the years?

   a. 4
   b. 5
   c. 6

3. How many times did Ford direct The Duke in cavalry uniform?

   a. 3
   b. 4
   c. 5

4. Ford, a war veteran, directed Wayne in how many military-related films?

   a. 3
   b. 4
   c. 5

5. How many Oscars did the Ford/Wayne combination win over the years?

   a. 2
   b. 3
   c. 4

6. What was the first John Ford directed film that The Duke appeared in?

   a. Stagecoach
   b. Salute
   c. Hangman's House

7. What was the last film that Ford directed Wayne in?

   a. The Searchers
   b. Donovan's Reef
   c. The Man Who Shot Liberty Valance

8. What part of the American West has come to be known as John Ford and John Wayne territory?

   a. Grants Pass, Oregon
   b. Death Valley, Utah
   c. Monument Valley, Arizona

9. In all but one of the John Ford movies listed below The Duke played the second male lead. Which film did he have the leading role?

   a. They Were Expendable
   b. The Man Who Shot Liberty Valance
   c. Fort Apache
   d. The Long Voyage Home
   e. The Searchers

10. What was The Duke's personal nickname for John Ford?

    a. Pappy
    b. The Admiral
    c. Jack
    d. Mr. Ford

11. What branch of the military did John Ford serve in during World War II? Hint: It was the same branch that The Duke asked Ford to get him into.

    a. U.S. Marines
    b. U.S. Air Force
    c. U.S. Navy
    d. U.S. Army

NUMBER TWO: THE EARLY MOVIE YEARS

1. What is the name of the first film that The Duke starred in?

   a. Stagecoach
   b. The Big Trail
   c. Red River

2. What was the name of his screen character in his first starring film?

   a. The Ringo Kid
   b. Quirt Evans
   c. Breck Coleman

3. All but one of the following were names of screen characters The Duke played in his early "B" Westerns. Which name is from his later career in "A" movies?

   a. Stony Brooke
   b. Tom Wayne
   c. Duke Slade
   d. Duke Gifford

4. Under what name did the Duke appear in his short-lived career as a singing cowboy?

   a. Singin' Sandy Saunders
   b. Singin' Stony Brooke
   c. Singin' Bob Seton
   d. Singin' Smith Ballew

5. The Duke played the same type of character in three early movie serials. The character he played was a:

   a. government agent
   b. pilot
   c. ship's captain

6. The Duke put on a Navy uniform in this film before World War II started. The 1936 film was:

   a. The Spoilers
   b. I Cover The War
   c. The Sea Spoilers

7. The Duke played a boxer in all but one of the following movies from the early part of his career. In which film did he not put on boxing gloves?

   a. Lady and Gent
   b. The Quiet Man
   c. The Life of Jimmy Dolan
   d. Conflict
   e. Idol of the Crowds

8. What was the name of The Duke's group of good guys in his early 1930's serials?

   a. The Three Musketeers
   b. Pals of the Saddle
   c. The Three Mesquiteers

9. What did The Duke take lessons for when making The Big Trail?

   a. Throwing a tomahawk
   b. Throwing a knife
   c. Riding a horse

10. The Duke appeared in what silent movie listed below?

    a. City Lights
    b. Hangman's House
    c. Three Girls Lost

11. In what film did The Duke have his first speaking part?

    a. The Big Trail
    b. The Westerner
    c. Salute

12. The Duke appeared with all but one of the future Grade A actresses named below during his early movie years. Which actress did The Duke star with in his later career?

    a. Loretta Young
    b. Barbara Stanwyck
    c. Jennifer Jones
    d. Marlene Dietrich

13. The Duke appeared with a former silent film beauty in a 1938 "B" Western Overland Stage Raiders. The lady was:

    a. Fay Wray
    b. Clara Bow
    c. Mary Pickford
    d. Louise Brooks

14. The Duke usually used his fists or his guns to dispose of the bad guys. However, in one early 1933 film he used a sword. The film in which The Duke was a swordsman was:

    a. Adventure's End
    b. The Three Musketeers
    c. The Man From Monterey

15. John Wayne's horse in six of his early films was a white stallion with an easy to remember name. The horse was called:

    a. Eagle
    b. Duke
    c. Blackie

16. What is the most memorable thing about The Duke's first starring-role film?

    a. It required a special screen.
    b. It was a box office flop.
    c. He changed his name to John Wayne for it.
    d. It was directed by Raoul Walsh.

NUMBER THREE: THE DUKE'S FAMILY ON FILM

1. The Duke's four children from his first marriage appeared with him in what film?

    a. The Alamo
    b. McLintock
    c. The Quiet Man
    d. Big Jake

2. The Duke's oldest son Michael played a guard in what Wayne film?

    a. The Sea Chase
    b. The Conqueror
    c. Blood Alley
    d. Brannigan

3. Two of The Duke's sons appeared with him in a later western film called:

    a. The Cowboys
    b. The Train Robbers
    c. Big Jake
    d. The Shootist

4. In another film, two of The Duke's children, his daughter and son, appeared with him in a 1960's film called:

    a. The Comancheros
    b. The Alamo
    c. North to Alaska
    d. Circus World

5. The Duke's youngest child, a daughter, appeared with him in a film called:

    a. Rooster Cogburn
    b. McQ
    c. The Shootist
    d. Chisum

NUMBER FOUR: THE DUKE MOVIE MISCELLANY

1. In the mega box office hit E.T., what John Wayne movie is the tiny space traveler watching on television while drinking beer?

   a. The High and the Mighty
   b. True Grit
   c. The Quiet Man
   d. The Alamo

2. The last movie actor to be shot and killed by The Duke in his last western was:

   a. Richard Boone
   b. Ron Howard
   c. Bruce Dern
   d. Hugh O'Brian

3. John Wayne movies over the years had many sport figures and singers appearing with The Duke. The lists below contain the names of athletes and singers who had roles in Wayne's films. Pick the name of the athlete or singer who did *not* appear with Wayne in a film.

Athlete	Singer
a. Roman Gabriel	d. Glen Campbell
b. Joe Namath	e. Bobby Vinton
c. Merlin Olsen	f. Bobby Rydall

4. Name the popular writer who had a bit part in a Wayne western then produced a television documentary about the experience.

   a. Henry Miller
   b. George Plimpton
   c. Truman Capote
   d. James Updike

5. Late in both their careers, The Duke appeared with Richard Boone in three films. Unfortunately for Boone Duke had to kill him in two films. The two films were:

   a. McQ and Brannigan
   b. El Dorado and Rio Lobo
   c. Big Jake and The Shootist

6. The Duke was a man who liked to wear hats. In all but one of the following movies he wore a coonskin cap. Name the movie that he did *not* wear a coonskin cap?

   a. The Fighting Kentuckian
   b. The Alamo
   c. The Shepherd of the Hills
   d. Allegheny Uprising

7. During his long film career, The Duke appeared as the tough, rugged American that he was. However, he did portray foreign nationals in a few films. The Duke played *all but one* of the foreigners shown below:

   a. A Swede
   b. A German
   c. A Mongol
   d. A Canadian

8. The Duke's longevity was unique among the super stars of our time. How many years did his movies appear on the screen?

   a. 45
   b. 48
   c. 50
   d. 52

9. Wayne played opposite many of Hollywood's most beautiful female stars. He did not appear with which one of the following leading ladies:

a. Joan Crawford
b. Lana Turner
c. Jane Russell
d. Sophia Loren

10. Wayne played Rooster Cogburn in two films. He also played another screen character in two different films. The character was Kirby York. The movies were:

a. The Horse Soldiers
b. Fort Apache
c. She Wore A Yellow Ribbon
d. Rio Grande

11. The Duke was nearly always the clean shaven hero in most of his films. He did, however, appear with a mustache in all but *one* of the following films:

a. Rio Grande
b. The Undefeated
c. The Shootist
d. She Wore A Yellow Ribbon
e. The Conqueror

12. During the 3-D craze of the early 1950's, John Wayne made one film in 3-D which was later released without the special three dimension process. The film was:

a. Big Jim McLain
b. Hondo
c. The High and the Mighty
d. Jet Pilot

13. The Duke was usually seen climbing onto his horse. In two films he climbed tall poles. Name the two movies that The Duke is up in the air on a pole:

a. Tycoon
b. North to Alaska
c. Hatari
d. Circus World

14. The Duke defended his country against both the Japanese and the Germans. How many war films did he appear in?

a. 15
b. 10
c. 11

15. The first John Wayne war film in which he saw combat against our enemies was:

a. The Long Voyage Home
b. The Fighting Seabees
c. Flying Tigers
d. Sands of Iwo Jima

16. The Duke's hair started thinning when he reached his early forties. He started to wear a hairpiece which provided a cosmetic fullness to his hairline. The first movie in which he appeared with his toupee was:

a. Sands of Iwo Jima
b. Operation Pacific
c. The Quiet Man
d. Rio Grande

The Duke played many roles in his long career. His first try at comedy was in 1943 when he starred opposite Jean Arthur in a film called The Lady Takes A Chance.

The shortest film title in The Duke's long career was MCQ, with three letters. The longest film title was The Man Who Shot Liberty Valance, which contains 27 letters in the title.

The Duke starred in three films with Rio in the title. The films were Rio Grande, Rio Bravo and Rio Lobo.

It is often said that art imitates life. In The Duke's last film, The Shootist, the audience learns from the dates on his tombstone that John Bernard Books is 57, going on 58 years of age, and dying of cancer. In real life, The Duke was operated on for cancer in 1964, at the age of 57.

At the time of his death, the Olympic Torch atop the Los Angeles Coliseum was lit in The Duke's honor.

In the later years of his career when discussing his performance in Red River, The Duke said that he played a heavy, a Captain Bligh type of character.

At the time of his first Oscar nomination for Sands of Iwo Jima, The Duke felt that his best work was in She Wore A Yellow Ribbon also made in 1949.

Duke in his last starring role as John Bernard Books, the dying gunfighter, in the 1976 film The Shootist.

131

17. The Duke was a very loyal friend who helped his friends when ever he could. In one instance, he was approached and asked to star in a television western series. He declined but had a young actor under contract that he recommended for the role. The series turned out to be a hit. The television show was:

a. Wagon Train
b. Gunsmoke
c. Bonanza
d. The Virginian

18. Film historians note that The Duke always played characters who were in control or in charge of events around him. The one role they cite that he wasn't in control was an early film called:

a. The Conqueror
b. Dakota
c. The Long Voyage Home
d. The Big Trail

19. The Great John Ford directed The Duke in four cavalry movies. However, only three have come to be known as Ford's Cavalry Trilogy. Which one of the films listed below is *not* considered part of the trilogy?

a. Rio Grande
b. Fort Apache
c. The Horse Soldiers
d. She Wore A Yellow Ribbon

20. The Duke and Maureen O'Hara once cast together made screen history. What film did they first appear together in?

a. The Quiet Man
b. Rio Grande
c. The Wings of Eagles
d. Big Jake

21. The last movie that Duke and Maureen O'Hara appeared in was:

a. McLintock
b. The Shootist
c. Big Jake
d. Rooster Cogburn

22. In the opening minutes of The Duke's last film the audience is treated to brief clips from Wayne's past western movies. Which one of the films listed below *did not* appear showing Wayne as an aging gunfighter:

a. Red River
b. Rio Bravo
c. Tall in the Saddle
d. Hondo
e. El Dorado

23. A John Wayne movie often co-starred young actors who went on to achieve later fame as serious actors. Name the young stage actor who first appeared in the movies with The Duke in 1948.

a. James Dean
b. James Caan
c. Montgomery Cliff

24. The Duke fought the Nazis during World War II in several films. However, he once played a German sea captain in a bit of unusual casting. The sea adventure was:

a. Reap the Wild Wind
b. The Sea Chase
c. In Harm's Way
d. Wake of the Red Witch

25. Another un-typical John Wayne film found The Duke speaking in a Swedish accent. This movie was:

a. Tycoon
b. The Shepherd of the Hills
c. The Long Voyage Home
d. Three Faces West

26. Perhaps the most unusual casting found The Duke playing an oriental in the forgettable movie called:

a. The Barbarian and the Geisha
b. Back to Bataan
c. Legend of the Lost
d. The Conqueror

27. The Duke was an outspoken anti-communist in real life. He got a chance to fight the communists in each of the following films except:

a. Big Jim McLain
b. Blood Alley
c. Trouble Along The Way
d. Jet Pilot

28. What was the name of The Duke's Yacht?

a. The Red Witch
b. The Glencairn
c. Wild Goose I
d. Wild Goose II

29. Veteran movie tough guy Lee Marvin appeared with The Duke in three films. In two of the three films, The Duke had to shoot him. Which film below does Lee Marvin live through?

a. The Comancheros
b. Donovan's Reef
c. The Man Who Shot Liberty Valance
d. The Shootist

30. The desperate cattle drive against great odds played the backdrop to several Wayne films. The Duke succeeded in each film except:

a. Red River
b. The Cowboys
c. Chisum

31. John Wayne was a personal friend of each of the movie stars listed below. Although they started their film careers about the same time "falling off horses" they never made a movie together. The Duke's friend that he never appeared with on screen was:

a. James Stewart
b. Robert Mitchum
c. Gary Cooper
d. Randolph Scott

32. Actors Bruce Cabot, Neville Brand and Howard Keel all appeared in John Wayne westerns. What is the common feature of their roles with The Duke?

a. each actor was killed in the movie
b. each actor played an outlaw
c. each actor played an Indian

33. The Duke was always the hero, well, almost always. In one film, he played a good man gone bad. His wrong decision causes the death of a young lady. In the end, he redeemed himself by saving the life of his former enemy. The movie was:

a. Pittsburgh
b. Reap the Wild Wind
c. Dark Command
d. Brannigan

34. In his long movie career, The Duke repeated many screen names. He used "Big Jake" twice, once in the film of the same name. The other film in which he was called Big Jake was:

a. McLintock
b. Rio Lobo
c. The Comancheros
d. The War Wagon

35. The Duke's second oldest son Patrick Wayne has been the only one so far to take up acting as a career. He appeared with his father in each of the following films except:

a. The Searchers
b. The Long Grey Line
c. Big Jake
d. McLintock

36. The Duke had many sidekicks in his film career. Which one of the fine character actors listed below *did not* appear with Wayne during his lifetime:

a. Walter Brennan
b. Walter Huston
c. Ward Bond
d. George Hayes

37. The Duke once appeared in a cameo spot in which the television audience only heard his voice. The show starred his best friend. The television show and friend was:

a. Gunsmoke – James Arness
b. Have Gun Will Travel – Richard Boone
c. Wagon Train – Ward Bond

38. The Duke's first appearance on television was on:

a. Gunsmoke
b. I Love Lucy
c. G.E. Theatre
d. Maude

39. The Duke had two members of the original Star Trek crew in his films. Which two?

    a. William Shatner
    b. George Takei
    c. Leonard Nemoy
    d. Jeffrey Hunter

40. Stagecoach in 1939 made John Wayne a Grade A movie star when he appeared on the screen as The Ringo Kid. What was the Ringo Kid's first name?

    a. John
    b. William
    c. Henry
    d. Ethan

41. The Duke survived in most of his films so that his death in a movie was almost a shock to the John Wayne fans watching the film. In one film we don't know if he lived or died. The film was:

    a. Island in the Sky
    b. Legend of the Lost
    c. The Sea Chase
    d. The Cowboys

42. In a light comedy that The Duke made in the late 1940's there was a memorable line spoken to him by his male co-star. It was "Rusty they're trying to make an actor out of you." The film in which this line was spoken was:

    a. A Lady Takes A Chance
    b. Without Reservations
    c. I Married a Woman

43. The Duke rode in the saddle for nearly fifty years. In one film he changed horses for a mule. The film was:

    a. Circus World
    b. Hatari
    c. Legend of the Lost

44. The Duke was the man's man, but in one movie he appeared without pants on. That movie was:

    a. Circus World
    b. The Greatest Story Ever Told
    c. Cast A Giant Shadow

45. The Duke's hair thinned midway through his long career. He did wear a toupee for the remainder of his acting career. However, in only one film did he actually appear without the hairpiece in the role of an aging aviator. The John Ford directed movie was:

    a. Jet Pilot
    b. Flying Leathernecks
    c. The Wings of Eagles
    d. The High and the Mighty

46. In which film shown below did The Duke have a one-line cameo role?

    a. How The West Was Won
    b. Cast A Giant Shadow
    c. The Greatest Story Ever Told
    d. The Longest Day

47. The Duke became a favorite with impressionists the older he got. Just about every impression of John Wayne has The Duke calling someone "pilgrim." What movie does this expression come from?

    a. True Grit
    b. Red River
    c. The Man Who Shot Liberty Valance
    d. The Shootist

48. Who was really the first singing cowboy in the movies?

    a. Roy Rogers
    b. Gene Autry
    c. Singing Sandy Saunders
    d. Tex Ritter

49. All but one of the following actors starred with The Duke in the early B western serial The Three Mesquiteers. Which actor was not in the cast?

    a. Ray Corrigan
    b. Johnny Mack Brown
    c. Robert Livingston
    d. Max Terhune

50. The Duke only appeared in one movie very early in his long career under his own name. This early movie was:

    a. The Big Trail
    b. Mother Machree
    c. Words and Music
    d. Girls Demand Excitement

51. The Duke spanks his lady love in what two films shown below?

    a. McLintock
    b. Big Jake
    c. The Quiet Man
    d. Donovan's Reef

52. Who was the original pick to play John Wayne's role in The Big Trail. Hint: They were close friends off-screen.

    a. Ward Bond
    b. Gary Cooper
    c. Lloyd Nolan
    d. Randolph Scott

NUMBER FIVE: THE DUKE IN LOVE

As he aged, John Wayne movies changed and the films' romantic interest shifted to a younger second male lead. However, The Duke still occasionally won the lady's heart. Match the film title with The Duke's romantic exploits on screen.

THE MOVIE	THE SCENARIO
1. Rooster Cogburn	a. The Duke loses his favorite girl to an eastern dude lawyer
2. The Cowboys	b. The Duke has an affair with a divorced Navy nurse
3. McLintock	c. The Duke is reunited with his long lost secret love
4. Circus World	d. The Duke is reconciled with his wife
5. Big Jake	e. The Duke is befriended by a widow and her son
6. In Harm's Way	f. The Duke returns home to help his wife with a family kidnapping
7. The Man Who Shot Liberty Valance	g. The Duke leaves his wife to lead a cattle drive
8. The Shootist	h. The Duke plans to marry his ex-commander's daughter
9. Donovan's Reef	i. The Duke falls in love with a French bar girl
10. North to Alaska	j. The Duke becomes friends with an old missionary's daughter

NUMBER SIX: THE DUKE'S LEADING LADIES

A. The Duke's leading ladies were among the most beautiful in Hollywood. See if you can match the lady with the film title.

LEADING LADY	MOVIE
1. Joan Crawford	a. Donovan's Reef
2. Paulette Goddard	b. Jet Pilot
3. Sophia Loren	c. The Sea Chase
4. Rita Hayworth	d. Hatari
5. Lana Turner	e. Circus World
6. Elsa Martinelli	f. Reap the Wild Wind
7. Ann-Margret	g. Legend of the Lost
8. Elizabeth Allen	h. Reunion in France
9. Angie Dickinson	i. Rio Bravo
10. Janet Leigh	j. The Train Robbers

B. Each of the leading ladies below appeared in at least two films with The Duke. See if you can pick each movie from the film titles taken from The Duke's screen credits.

1. Donna Reed
2. Gail Russell
3. Lauren Bacall
4. Vera Ralston
5. Patricia Neal

a. In Harm's Way
b. Trouble Along the Way
c. Angel and the Badman
d. Operation Pacific
e. They Were Expendable
f. Wake of the Red Witch
g. The Shootist
h. Dakota
i. Blood Alley
j. The Fighting Kentuckian

C. Some of the Duke's leading ladies appeared in more than two films with him over the years. See if you can match the film titles to the leading lady shown below:

LEADING LADY	THE FILMS
1. Susan Hayward	(a) Stagecoach Alleghany Uprising Dark Command The High and the Mighty
2. Claire Trevor	(b) Seven Sinners The Spoilers Pittsburgh
3. Marlene Dietrich	(c) Reap the Wild Wind The Fighting Seabees The Conqueror
4. Vera Miles	(d) Rio Grande The Quiet Man The Wings of Eagles McLintock Big Jake
5. Maureen O'Hara	(e) The Searchers The Man Who Shot Liberty Valance Hellfighters

NUMBER SEVEN: THE INDESTRUCTIBLE DUKE

A. The Duke was indestructible and survived the cinematic forces against him in almost all his films. So, a movie in which John Wayne dies is noteworthy. As a John Wayne fan you should know every movie he died in and the cause of his death. Match the movie titles below with the cause of his demise.

MOVIE TITLE	HOW THE DUKE DIED
1. Reap The Wild Wind	(a) shot in the back by a rustler
2. The Shootist	(b) died of old age
3. The Cowboys	(c) stabbed with a lance
4. The Man Who Shot Liberty Valance	(d) shot through the heart by a sniper
5. The Fighting Seabees	(e) drowned by a giant squid
6. Sands of Iwo Jima	(f) died of multiple gun wounds
7. The Alamo	(g) drowned as ship drops off ledge
8. Wake of the Red Witch	(h) shot in the chest by a sniper

NOTE: In The Sea Chase we really don't know if The Duke lives or drowns with Lana Turner aboard his ship. The film ends with the suggestion that he lived and spent the rest of the war in neutral Scandinavia.

B. John Wayne came close to death in many films. Match the reason that he survived in the film with the movie title.

REASON	MOVIE TITLE
1. He is ordered to get back on the military plane.	(a) Rio Bravo
2. He is ordered to the rear to guard the supply wagons.	(b) Hondo
3. He is rescued by friends from being kidnapped.	(c) Angel and the Badman
4. The old marshal shoots three gunmen facing him.	(d) They Were Expendable
5. The Texas lawman kills the outlaw about to shoot him.	(e) The Comancheros
6. His partner's girlfriend saves their lives.	(f) True Grit
7. The chief is shown a small boy's photograph.	(g) The Long Voyage Home
8. His girlfriend throws a flowerpot through the window.	(h) Fort Apache
9. The villain's mother hits his gun as he is about to shoot The Duke.	(i) The Green Berets
10. His company sergeant takes the lead and is caught in a deadly booby trap.	(j) Dark Command

C. John Wayne survived most of his films with little injury to his screen character. However, in some films The Duke does get injured. Match the injury to the movie he appeared in:

INJURY	MOVIE TITLE
1. The Duke breaks a leg after parachuting to ground.	a) Hondo
2. The Duke breaks his arm and later loses a leg.	b) The Wings of Eagles
3. The Duke falls down a flight of stairs and breaks his neck.	c) Red River
4. The Duke is shot in the hand which later becomes infected.	d) Big Jake
5. The Duke is shot in the side in a gun fight.	e) In Harm's Way
6. The Duke is shot in the leg during a shootout.	f) They Were Expendable
7. The Duke is stabbed with a knife during a fight for his life.	g) The Longest Day

NUMBER EIGHT: THE DUKE GOES TO WAR

Match the military character's name with the movie The Duke starred in:

NAME	MOVIE TITLE
1. Jim Gordon	a) The Green Berets
2. Joseph Madden	b) Cast a Giant Shadow
3. Rusty Ryan	c) The Fighting Seabees
4. Kirby York	d) Flying Tigers
5. Nathan Brittles	e) Flying Leathernecks
6. John M. Stryker	f) In Harm's Way
7. Duke Gifford	g) Operation Pacific
8. Dan Kirby	h) The Horse Soldiers
9. Frank W. Wead	i) The Wings of Eagles
10. John Marlowe	j) She Wore A Yellow Ribbon
11. Benjamin Vandervoort	k) The Longest Day
12. Rockwell Torrey	l) They Were Expendable
13. Mike Kirby	m) Sands of Iwo Jima
14. Mike Randolph	n) Rio Grande
15. Wedge Donovan	o) Back to Bataan

NUMBER NINE: THE DUKE IN UNIFORM

John Wayne wore many uniforms and held different ranks through the years. Match the military rank with the war movie he starred in:

RANK	MOVIE TITLE
1. Admiral	a) Seven Sinners
2. General	b) In Harm's Way
3. Lieutenant Colonel	c) Cast a Giant Shadow
4. Sergeant	d) Fort Apache
5. Captain	e) The Longest Day
6. Colonel	f) Sands of Iwo Jima
7. Lieutenant	g) Back to Bataan
8. Lieutenant Commander	h) Flying Leathernecks
9. Major	j) Operation Pacific
10. Commander	k) The Wings of Eagles

NUMBER TEN: THE DUKE OUT OF UNIFORM

John Wayne played mostly cowboys and military heros. However, in his long movie career he appeared in many other character roles. Match The Duke's screen occupation with the correct movie title:

OCCUPATION	MOVIE TITLE
1. football coach	a) Three Faces West
2. professional boxer	b) Lady From Louisiana
3. coal miner	c) The Shepherd of the Hills
4. airline pilot	d) Lady for a Night
5. mountaineer	e) Pittsburgh
6. pharmacist	f) The Quiet Man
7. engineer	g) Legend of the Lost
8. desert guide	h) Tycoon
9. oil firefighter	i) Trouble Along the Way
10. city cop	j) In Old California
11. Mississippi gambler	k) Hellfighters
12. lawyer	l) The High and the Mighty
13. farmer	m) Brannigan
14. circus owner	n) Hatari
15. big game hunter	o) Circus World
16. gold miner	p) The Spoilers

NUMBER ELEVEN: THE DUKE ON LOCATION

While the American west was John Wayne's most natural and typical background for his movies, he did appear in more exotic locales. Match the background with the movie title:

BACKGROUND	MOVIE TITLE
1. South American Andes	a) Circus World
2. East Africa	b) Legend of the Lost
3. Sahara Desert	c) Tycoon
4. Europe	d) Hatari
5. Japan	e) The Green Berets
6. Labrador	f) Big Jim McLain
7. Hawaii	g) Island in the Sky
8. Russia	h) The Barbarian and the Geisha
9. China	i) Jet Pilot
10. Vietnam	j) Brannigan
11. England	k) Blood Alley
12. Phillippines	l) They Were Expendable

Duke as the young handsome leading man early in his career.

The Comancheros made in 1961 marked a turning point in The Duke's acting career. At the age of 54, The Duke would no longer play the primary romantic lead in his films.

The Duke's ad-lib at receiving his Oscar for True Grit: "Wow, if I'd known that, I'd put on an eyepatch thirty-five years earlier."

The Duke's father gave him advice which he honored throughout his life. "Always keep your word, never intentionally insult anyone, and don't go around looking for trouble."

The Duke appeared in a cameo role as an officer in the 82nd Airborne Division in the film The Longest Day. He wore the West Point ring of General James Gavin for luck.

The Duke turned down the lead in Dirty Harry which was to become a big hit for Clint Eastwood because of its violence and vulgar language.

The Duke was asked to star in TV's Gunsmoke. He refused but convinced the producers to use James Arness. He appeared on the first show asking for fan support for the series.

The Duke's most controversial film was thought to be The Green Berets made at the height of anti-Viet Nam feeling in this country.

The Duke smoked five packs of cigarettes a day before his operation for cancer. He started smoking when he was twelve years old. In the 1950's he appeared in advertisements for Camels his brand at the time.

NUMBER TWELVE: IMAGES OF THE DUKE

Every John Wayne movie is filled with strong, dramatic images. Match the image with the movie title from some of The Duke's many screen credits.

THE IMAGE	THE FILM
1. An old marshal with an eyepatch	a) The Searchers
2. The Marines raising the American flag.	b) The Sons of Katie Elder
3. A fatal knockout in a boxing match	c) The Cowboys
4. A silver retirement watch	d) The Man Who Shot Liberty Valance
5. An Indian chief's scalp	e) Sands of Iwo Jima
6. Three bullets saved in his hat	f) The Shootist
7. A rifle shot from a dark alley	g) McLintock
8. A showdown in a saloon	h) The Quiet Man
9. A violent stampede	i) She Wore A Yellow Ribbon
10. A deadly Indian victory	j) True Grit
11. Waves of soldiers attacking the fort	k) Stagecoach
12. Burning coals placed in his hands	l) Red River
13. A muddy fight up and down the hill	m) The Alamo
14. Fighting a giant squid	n) Fort Apache
15. Hitting a man with his Winchester	o) The Horse Soldiers
16. Staggering into the saloon with a baby	p) Rio Grande
17. Slumped across a moving tractor	q) Rio Bravo
18. Clearing out a bar	r) Reap the Wild Wind
19. Escorting on foot his wife's wagon	s) Three Godfathers
20. A shot in the back	t) Hondo
21. The gunman watching from the hill	u) The Fighting Seabees

NUMBER THIRTEEN: THE DUKE'S SCREEN TALK

Audiences were never disappointed seeing "A John Wayne Movie" since The Duke always gave his fans what they wanted. The Duke dominated the movie and its action. See if you can match the dialogue from the movie with the title of the film.

THE DIALOGUE	THE MOVIE
1. "That'll be the day."	a) The Quiet Man
2. "Saddle-up."	b) She Wore A Yellow Ribbon
3. "Never say you're sorry, it's a sign of weakness."	c) The Searchers
4. "You say three, mister, and you'll never hear the man count ten."	d) Sands of Iwo Jima
5. "Are you all right, Pilgrim?"	e) The Man Who Shot Liberty Valance
6. "Now listen, little sister."	f) True Grit
7. "I haven't lost my temper in forty years."	g) The Shootist
8. "Everybody gets dead. It was his turn."	h) McLintock
9. "You want that gun? Pick it up, I wish you would."	i) Hondo
10. "I won't be wronged, I won't be insulted, I won't be laid a hand on."	j) Rio Bravo

NUMBER FOURTEEN:
MILESTONES BY AGE IN THE DUKE'S MOVIE CAREER

AGE	MILESTONE
21	The Duke appears in his first John Ford film, Hangman's House, a silent movie, in 1928. The friendship and film partnership with Ford begins.
23	The Duke had his first starring role in the 1930 film The Big Trail. He was also given his movie name, John Wayne. The movie was a flop and Wayne was to work in "B" and "C" films, mostly westerns for the next nine years.
32	John Ford picks Wayne for the role of the Ringo Kid in Stagecoach. The film was Wayne's ticket to "A" movies and his place as America's personal cowboy hero. The year was 1939.
41	The Duke plays the part of Thomas Dunson in Red River in 1948. This part showed the critics that Wayne could act without John Ford directing him. It revitalized Wayne's career and gave him a character he was to play for the remainder of his long career.
42	In 1949, The Duke received his first Academy Award nomination for Sands of Iwo Jima. He always thought he did better in She Wore A Yellow Ribbon.
49	The Duke works for John Ford again and gives his greatest screen performance in The Searchers, made in 1956.
53	After a decade of planning, Wayne made The Alamo in 1960. It was his personal dream to make a film honoring America and its early heroes. The film was a box-office disappointment and nearly bankrupt The Duke after 32 years in the film business.
58	The Duke makes The Sons of Katie Elder in 1965 after having his left lung removed for cancer. This film proved that he was not considering retirement.

62	The Duke stars as Rooster Cogburn in True Grit and gives his career a boost in 1969. More importantly, he wins the Academy Award for Best Actor, the capstone performance of his long acting career.
69	In 1976, The Duke made his last film, The Shootist. This film, destined to stand among the other classic Wayne westerns, is about an aging gunfighter dying of cancer. Wayne's performance is magnificent.

NUMBER FIFTEEN: THE IRON DUKE

The Duke came from humble beginnings, having to work his way through college with scholarships and odd jobs. After leaving college, he worked even harder at his new chosen profession, the movies. The determination and drive that John Wayne so forcefully projected on the big screen was present in real life and, amazingly, he starred in as many as seven major films in a single year (1942). In 1933, during his lean years as a "B" western star, The Duke made eleven films. Included in this total is a twelve-part serial called The Three Musketeers. The driving force for this incredible output was Wayne's need to provide for a growing family and an even stronger desire to achieve which John Ford instilled in his young protege. To watch these action films and realize that The Duke was doing his own stunt work while working 20 hour days, you can appreciate how strong and durable John Wayne was and why the screen legend merely reflected Wayne the man.

The Duke was 34 years old with four young children, and an old college football injury when World War II started. He never served in the military but did visit troops in the Pacific during the war.

The Duke had four children from his first marriage. At the time of his death these children had given him twenty-one grandchildren.

John Wayne was a founder and three-term president of the Motion Picture Alliance for the Preservation of American Ideals, an anti-communist organization founded to keep communist influence out of motion pictures.

In the present era of million dollar contracts, it was John Wayne who was the first major star to receive a million dollars and a percentage of the profits for a film.

The Duke's female companion for the remainder of his life following his separation from Pilar was his personal secretary Pat Stacy.

General Douglas MacArthur once said of The Duke "You represent the cavalry officer better than any man who wears a uniform."

The Duke once finished second to Abraham Lincoln in a 1970's poll of history's most famous Americans.

The Duke recorded an album in 1973, his first, entitled "America, Why I Love Her."

A young Duke Wayne with the look that had become America's symbol for its cowboy hero.

Real Name:	Marion Michael Morrison
Date of Birth:	May 26, 1907
Place of Birth:	Winterset, Iowa
Father's Name:	Clyde L. Morrison
Mother's Name:	Mary A. Brown
Brother's Name:	Robert Morrison
Nationality:	Scotch/English, Irish
Color of Eyes:	Blue
Color of Hair:	Brown
Height:	6'4"
Weight:	212 lbs +
Number of Times Married:	Three
Wives' Names:	Josephine Saenz
	Esperanza Bauer
	Pilar Palette
Number of Children:	Seven
Children's Names:	Michael
	Antonia
	Patrick
	Melinda
	Aissa
	John Ethan
	Marisa
First Movie Made:	Mother Machree, 1928
Last Movie Made:	The Shootist, 1976
Favorite Director:	John Ford
Number of Films Made:	153
His Favorite Films:	The Quiet Man, The Searchers
Number of Oscar Nominations:	Two
Films Nominated for:	Sands of Iwo Jima
	True Grit
Oscar Winning Performance:	Rooster Cogburn in True Grit, 1970
First Starring Role:	1930, The Big Trail
Years in Top Ten Box Office:	24 (1949 to 1973)
Closest Friend:	Ward Bond
Name of Movie Production Co.	Batjac Productions
Number of Movies Directed:	Two – The Alamo, The Green Berets
Most Expensive Film Produced:	The Alamo – $12,000,000 +
Executive at Batjac Productions:	Michael Wayne, his oldest son
Estimated Box Office Gross:	$700 Million +
Favorite Drinks:	Bourbon, Scotch, Tequila
Political Party:	Republican Party
Last Public Appearance:	1979 Academy Awards Show, (April 9,)
Date Died:	June 11, 1979
Age at Death:	72
Place Buried:	Pacific View Memorial Park, Newport Beach, California

Favorite Epitaph:	"Feo, Fuerte y Formal" Spanish proverb meaning "He was ugly, strong and had dignity."
Religion:	Raised Presbyterian but converted to Roman Catholic before his death.
Nickname:	Duke
Last Film Working on:	Beau James – never filmed.
High School Attended:	Glendale High School, Glendale, California
College Attended:	USC
Sport/Position Played:	Football/Tackle
Fraternity:	SigmaChi
Stand-in/Stuntman:	Chuck Roberson

THE JOHN WAYNE FILMOGRAPHY

Author's note: Depending on the reference source used you will read that John Wayne's first screen credit was one of the following five films: BROWN OF HARVARD, FOUR SONS, THE DROP KICK, HANGMAN'S HOUSE or MOTHER MACHREE. For the record THE DUKE's film career includes all these films but in the first three he had bit parts and no screen credit. In HANGMAN'S HOUSE he played a spectator at a horse race, again without credit. In MOTHER MACHREE he had a brief appearance in a walk-on part without screen credit. THE DUKE's first film in which he had dialogue and screen credit was WORDS AND MUSIC in 1929. He appeared in the screen credits under his real name as Duke Morrison. He appeared in four other films SALUTE, MEN WITHOUT WOMEN, ROUGH ROMANCE and CHEER UP AND SMILE before he got his big break and the starring role in the 1930 film THE BIG TRAIL. For the role of Breck Coleman, Duke Morrison became JOHN WAYNE and changed the history of motion pictures forever. I have decided to start THE DUKE's filmography with HANGMAN'S HOUSE the 1928 film directed by John Ford since it was the first time that John Wayne's presence was noticed by movie goers and directors alike. Finally, the films shown in caps represent milestone films in The Duke's long film career.

1928	Hangman's House
1928	Mother Machree
1929	Words and Music
1929	Salute
1930	Men Without Women
1930	Rough Romance
1930	Cheer Up And Smile
1930	THE BIG TRAIL
1931	Three Girls Lost
1931	Girls Demand Excitement
1931	Men Are Like That
1931	Range Feud
1931	Maker of Men
1932	Texas Cyclone
1932	Two-Fisted Law
1932	Lady and Gent
1932	Shadow of the Eagle

1932	The Hurricane Express
1932	Ride Him Cowboy
1932	The Big Stampede
1932	Haunted Gold
1933	The Telegraph Trail
1933	Central Airport
1933	The Three Musketeers
1933	His Private Secretary
1933	Somewhere in Sonora
1933	The Life of Jimmy Dolan
1933	Baby Face
1933	The Man from Monterey
1933	Riders of Destiny
1933	College Coach
1933	Sagebrush Trail
1934	The Lucky Texan
1934	West of the Divide
1934	Blue Steel
1934	The Man from Utah
1934	Randy Rides Alone
1934	The Star Packer
1934	The Trail Beyond
1934	The Lawless Frontier
1934	'Neath Arizona Skies
1935	Texas Terror
1935	Rainbow Valley
1935	The Desert Trail
1935	The Dawn Rider
1935	Paradise Canyon
1935	Westward Ho
1935	The New Frontier
1935	The Lawless Range
1936	The Oregon Trail
1936	The Lawless Nineties
1936	King of the Pecos
1936	The Lonely Trail
1936	Winds of the Wasteland
1936	The Sea Spoilers
1936	Conflict
1937	California Straight Ahead
1937	I Cover the War
1937	Idol of the Crowds
1937	Adventure's End
1937	Born to the West
1938	Pals of the Saddle
1938	Overland Stage Riders

1938	Santa Fe Stampede
1938	Red River Range
1939	The Night Riders
1939	Three Texas Steers
1939	Wyoming Outlaw
1939	New Frontier
1939	STAGECOACH
1939	Allegheny Uprising
1940	The Dark Command
1940	Three Faces West
1940	THE LONG VOYAGE HOME
1940	Seven Sinners
1941	A Man Betrayed
1941	Lady from Louisiana
1941	The Shepherd of the Hills
1942	Lady for a Night
1942	Reap the Wild Wind
1942	The Spoilers
1942	In Old California
1942	Flying Tigers
1942	Reunion in France
1942	Pittsburgh
1943	A Lady Takes A Chance
1943	In Old Oklahoma
1944	The Fighting Seabees
1944	Tall in the Saddle
1945	Flame of the Barbary Coast
1945	Back to Bataan
1945	THEY WERE EXPENDABLE
1945	Dakota
1946	Without Reservations
1947	Angel and the Badman
1947	Tycoon
1948	FORT APACHE
1948	RED RIVER
1949	THREE GODFATHERS
1949	Wake of the Red Witch
1949	The Fighting Kentuckian

1949	SHE WORE A YELLOW RIBBON
1949	SANDS OF IWO JIMA**
1950	RIO GRANDE
1951	Operation Pacific
1951	Flying Leathernecks
1952	THE QUIET MAN
1952	Big Jim McLain
1953	Trouble Along the Way
1953	Island in the Sky
1953	Hondo
1954	The High and the Mighty
1955	The Sea Chase
1955	Blood Alley
1956	The Conqueror
1956	THE SEARCHERS
1957	The Wings of Eagles
1957	Jet Pilot
1957	Legend of the Lost
1958	I Married A Woman*
1958	The Barbarian and the Geisha
1959	Rio Bravo
1959	The Horse Soldiers
1960	The Alamo
1960	North to Alaska
1961	The Comancheros
1962	The Man Who Shot Liberty Valance
1962	Hatari
1962	How The West Was Won
1962	The Longest Day*
1963	Donovan's Reef
1963	McLintock
1964	Circus World
1965	The Greatest Story Ever Told*
1965	In Harm's Way
1965	The Sons of Katie Elder
1966	Cast A Giant Shadow*
1967	The War Wagon
1967	El Dorado
1968	The Green Berets

1969	Hellfighters
1969	TRUE GRIT***
1969	The Undefeated
1970	Chisum
1970	Rio Lobo
1971	Big Jake
1972	The Cowboys
1973	The Train Robbers
1973	Cahill: United States Marshal
1974	McQ
1975	Brannigan
1975	Rooster Cogburn
1976	THE SHOOTIST

    * = Cameo Role
  ** = Academy Award Nomination
*** = Academy Award Winner

Note: In a 1931 film The Deceiver not shown above Wayne played a corpse. Also, to get an accurate count of the number of movies John Wayne made depends on how you count them. I chose to count individual movie titles. The total is 153 films made between 1928 and 1976.

The Duke as he is about to engage in his last screen gunfight in The Shootist.

In 1973, The Duke received The Veterans of Foreign Wars highest award their National Americanism Gold Medal.

When The Duke visited the troops in Viet Nam in 1966, he received a Montagnard tribal bracelet which he wore on his right wrist for the remainder of his life.

The Duke's first wife was a devout Roman Catholic. He married her in the Catholic Church and raised their four children as Catholics. However, the Duke was raised as a Presbyterian and was not a churchgoer. He is said to have converted to Catholicism several days before his death.

In his last public appearance on April 9, 1979, The Duke presented the Academy Award for Best Picture to The Deer Hunter. It is ironic that Wayne, who did not personally like the movie, is mentioned in the film during a scene in which Robert DeNiro is belittling actor John Cazale for never being prepared for their hunting trips. DeNiro says: "....all he's got is that stupid gun he carries around like John Wayne."

Upon his death, a Japanese newspaper ran as its front page headline "Mr. America is Dead."

The special gold medal issued by Congress to The Duke was introduced in Congress by his friend Senator Barry Goldwater. The gold medal bears the likeness of Wayne as Davy Crockett on one side. The other side contains the image of Monument Valley. The inscription reads "John Wayne, American."

NOTES

ANSWERS

1. b. Winterset, Iowa
2. b. May 26, 1907
3. b. Marion Michael Morrison
4. c. Iowa
5. c. Nebraska
6. d. All of the above
7. c. Druggist
8. c. named after pet airedale terrier
9. b. Glendale High School
10. c. 6 feet, 4 inches tall
11. d. Naval Academy at Annapolis
12. b. University of Southern California
13. c. Football
14. b. Football tackle
15. b. Sigmi Chi
16. b. He was a Pre-law major.
17. a. He suffered an ankle injury.
18. c. He attended until his sophomore year.
19. b. Tom Mix
20. c. Fox Studios
21. b. worked as fourth assistant propman
22. a. Hangman's House
23. a. Words and Music
24. b. Duke Morrison
25. c. Raoul Walsh
26. b. The Big Trail
27. b. Gary Cooper

28. b. Named after "Mad Anthony Wayne" the American Revolutionary War Hero. First name John just sounded strong.
29. c. He was married three times.
30. b. The Duke's wives were all Hispanic.
31. c. The Duke had seven children.
32. c. The Duke had 21 grandchildren.
33. d. He was rejected for all of the above.
34. a. The Duke made 153 films.
35. b. Ken Maynard
36. b. The Duke was never a screenwriter.
37. c. The Duke was in top ten 24 years.
38. b. form his own production company
39. b. Wake of the Red Witch
40. c. Angel and the Badman
41. b. The Alamo
42. b. The Duke was nominated twice.
43. c. The Sons of Katie Elder
44. b. Rooster Cogburn—True Grit
45. c. The Duke's last film was The Shootist.
46. c. The Duke wore a toupee.
47. b. A Gold Medal minted in his honor which read JOHN WAYNE, AMERICAN.

ANSWERS
To The Major Classics
NUMBER ONE: THE SEARCHERS

1. b. He is returning from the Civil War.
2. a. Texas
3. b. The Confederate Side
4. c. He was a Sergeant.
5. b. California
6. c. 180 Double Eagle Gold Coins
7. c. He gave her his war medal.
8. b. She tenderly and lovingly strokes his coat.
9. b. The Indians have stolen some cattle.
10. d. Comanche
11. b. Topsy
12. c. Ethan shoots the dead Indian's eyes out.
13. b. Ethan buried his niece Lucy in it.
14. b. A piece of Debbie's apron
15. b. Chief Scar
16. b. Big Shoulders
17. b. He is wearing Ethan's Confederate War Medal around his neck.
18. c. He is shot in the shoulder with an arrow.
19. b. Martin Pauley kills Chief Scar.
20. b. Ethan scalps him.
21. b. Ethan takes her into his arms.
22. c. five years.

NUMBER TWO: RED RIVER

1. b. a bracelet
2. c. He takes it from the arm of a dead Indian brave.
3. b. seven
4. c. Missouri
5. b. a small pistol
6. b. Dunson teaches him how to fast draw.
7. c. He is cash poor after the Civil War.
8. b. They shoot a tin can in the air.
9. c. pots and pans falling loudly from the chuckwagon
10. b. He wants to whip him.
11. c. He stays awake at night watching them.
12. b. Dunson wants to hang two runaways.
13. c. Matthew Garth
14. b. Dunson tells him to watch behind you because one time I'll be there.
15. c. Tess attempts to talk him out of killing Matt.
16. c. Dunson is hit in the left side.
17. b. Dunson grazes his right cheek.
18. b. Dunson tells him to change the branding irons.

NUMBER THREE: SHE WORE A YELLOW RIBBON

1. c. six days left
2. b. Indiana
3. c. He visits her grave and talks with her.
4. b. take a patrol to warn the settlers while escorting the commandant's kin to the stagecoach stop.
5. c. The troopers give him a silver watch with an inscription.
6. c. Brittles leads a surprise raid on the Indian camp to stampede their horses.
7. b. He breaks the arrow and spits on it.
8. c. He has been appointed Chief of Civilian Scouts.
9. b. California
10. c. seven
11. b. He calls him by his first name.
12. c. Wayne played a character older than himself.
13. b. She has a sweetheart in the cavalry.
14. d. General Lee
15. b. He smells his breath.
16. c. Ben Johnson
17. b. Tom Tyler

NUMBER FOUR: TRUE GRIT

1. a. left
2. b. during a Civil War battle
3. c. He killed 23 men.
4. c. Old Bo
5. b. General Sterling Price
6. c. Little Sister
7. b. He owned an eating place in Illinois.
8. c. Nola and Horace
9. b. Captain Charles Quantrill
10. c. Rooster shot him in the lip.
11. b. Le Boeff is a Texas Ranger.
12. c. He puts Bo's reins in his mouth and charges with both guns firing.
13. b. "Fill your hand, you son of a bitch."
14. c. He kills Ned Pepper before he can shoot Rooster.
15. b. a place in her family cemetery plot.

NUMBER FIVE: STAGECOACH

1. a. his saddle and rifle
2. c. to get the Plummer brothers
3. a. none
4. b. He sees Apache smoke signals.
5. b. Overland Stage Line
6. b. The arming lever has a round loop.
7. c. Three bullets in his hat.
8. b. three brothers, one dies in the bar
9. c. a prostitute
10. c. They ride off together in a buckboard to his ranch.
11. b. Lloyd Nolan
12. c. Gone With The Wind
13. b. Thomas Mitchell
14. b. John Carradine
15. c. Monument Valley, Arizona/Utah
16. b. The writer was Ernest Haycox.

NUMBER SIX: THE SHOOTIST

1. b. He is dying of cancer.
2. c. William Hickok
3. c. Moses, the stable owner, finds Books' name on his saddle.
4. b. He bought a newspaper
5. a. two
6. b. He asks to let him run errands for him.
7. b. You have to watch for the amateur.
8. c. Old Dollar
9. b. She wants him to marry her so she can earn money as his widow.
10. c. He makes arrangements for his funeral and tombstone.
11. c. Books had killed his brother.
12. a. He was 58 years old.
13. b. He left his goldwatch and money.
14. c. The bartender shoots him in the back.

NUMBER SEVEN: THE QUIET MAN

1. c. He is holding an apple.
2. b. He was a professional boxer who killed someone in a fight.
3. a. Pittsburgh
4. c. Sean wants to buy his family cottage to live in.
5. b. He first sees her in an open field herding her sheep.
6. c. He outbids him for his family cottage.
7. c. Will thinks he will be able to marry the rich widow.
8. d. all of the above
9. b. He killed a boxer in a fight.
10. c. Mary Kate leaves him early in the morning.
11. b. She is hiding in a railroad car.
12. b. He walks her back to her brother's farm.
13. b. 350 pounds
14. b. Sean throws the money into a fire.
15. c. Sean knocks Will through the door of the pub.

NUMBER EIGHT: RIO GRANDE

1. c. He hears his name called at inspection.
2. b. He failed mathematics at West Point.
3. c. He will expect twice as much from him.
4. c. She wants her son released from the army.
5. b. Kirby ordered her plantation burned.
6. c. fifteen years
7. c. Bridesdale
8. b. an arsonist
9. b. I'll Take You Home Again, Kathleen.
10. c. a confederate ten dollar bill
11. c. General Sheridan
12. b. chase the Apaches into Mexico
13. c. locate and defend the kidnapped children
14. b. He is shot in the shoulder with an arrow.
15. c. General Sheridan orders the band to play Dixie.

NUMBER NINE: SANDS OF IWO JIMA

1. a. Sergeant Major
2. b. He was found drunk.
3. c. Stryker beat him in a boxing match.
4. b. Stryker knew his father.
5. c. It was a family tradition.
6. b. He makes him practice to a polka recording.
7. c. "Saddle up"
8. b. Tarawa
9. c. He knocks him to the ground as a grenade explodes.
10. b. Stryker learned that Thomas got one of his men killed
11. c. His wife left him and took their son.
12. b. giving her money for her baby
13. c. He is shot to death by a sniper.
14. b. Forrest Tucker
15. a. raising the flag on Mount Suribachi

NUMBER TEN: THREE GODFATHERS

1. a. He has a funny sounding first name.
2. b. to rob the bank
3. c. He shoots a hole in their water bag.
4. b. the wounded Abilene Kid
5. c. a group of deputies
6. c. a pregnant woman in a covered wagon
7. b. helping the woman have the baby
8. b. the Mexican
9. b. Hightower was the first to find the mother.
10. c. New Jerusalem
11. a. John Wayne
12. b. the town Marshal
13. c. He refused to break his promise to the baby's mother.
14. b. Christmas
15. c. Harry Carey, Jr.

ANSWERS
To The Minor Classics
NUMBER ELEVEN: THEY WERE EXPENDABLE

1. c. The fall of the Philippines is the background to this excellent war film.
2. b. Rusty (Wayne) is filling out his transfer papers. He then throws it away.
3. a. Rusty commands a P-T Boat.
4. c. Returning naval veteran Robert Montgomery played the lead role of John Brickley.
5. b. The squadron is ordered to transport the Admiral's messages between the islands.
6. c. Rusty's wounded hand becomes badly infected.
7. b. A young and beautiful Donna Reed played the part.
8. c. In the film the squadron is asked to transport Gen. Douglas A. MacArthur.

9. a. Rusty's ship is blown up and sunk by a Japanese airplane.
10. c. They are ordered flown to the States to train others for combat.
11. b. There were four boats in Motor Torpedo Squadron No. 3.
12. a. Rusty's right hand is hit by a Japanese airplane's bullet.
13. c. Nurse Sandy Davyss pulls off The Duke's pants.
14. b. Sandy is from Iowa and Rusty tells her he is from upper New York State where the apples grow.
15. c. Rusty tries to get off the plane to give his place to a married Air Force Captain.

NUMBER TWELVE: FORT APACHE

1. a. Lt. Col. Thursday lives by the book of military rules.
2. c. Shirley Temple in one of her few adult roles played Henry Fonda's daughter.
3. c. Her full name is Philadelphia Thursday.
4. d. Capt. York visits Cochise's camp to ask him to attend a pow-wow with Col. Thursday.
5. b. Col. Thursday insults the great Cochise and orders him back to the reservation.

6. c. Thursday's contempt leads to his death.
7. d. Capt. York is ordered to the rear to guard the supply wagons.
8. c. Capt. York never lied to Cochise.
9. b. Cochise throws the regimental standard at York's feet then rides off.
10. a. York agrees with the newsman's version of the fatal battle even though false.

NUMBER THIRTEEN: THE MAN WHO SHOT LIBERTY VALANCE

1. a. Tom Doniphon finds Stoddard beaten and half dead.
2. c. Doniphon calls him pilgrim.
3. b. Valance trips Stoddard who is carrying Doniphon's steak.
4. c. Stoddard recognizes Liberty's whip.
5. c. Stoddard is trained as a lawyer.
6. b. Doniphon gives the pilgrim a lesson in how to shoot a pistol.
7. b. Liberty called Stoddard dude.
8. c. Doniphon shoots and kills Liberty with a shot from a darkened alley.
9. b. Tom gets drunk in town then goes home and sets fire to his ranch house.
10. c. Tom tells him that he killed Liberty with a rifle shot from the alley.
11. c. Woody Strode played Pompey who worked for Doniphon.

NUMBER FOURTEEN: RIO BRAVO

1. c. Chance was hit by his former deputy.
2. b. Chance tried to stop Dude from taking the dollar from the spittoon.
3. c. Dude fell in love with a bad woman.
4. c. The old deputy's name is Stumpy.
5. b. Chance only has two deputies to guard his prisoner Joe Burdette.
6. b. Ward Bond played the role of Pat Wheeler.
7. c. Wheeler is shot in the back and killed by a hired killer.
8. b. Dude notices the blood dripping on the bar from above.
9. c. Chance hits one of the gang in the face with his Winchester.
10. b. The young lady is nicknamed Feathers.
11. c. Chance tells Colorado he always carries his loaded Winchester.
12. c. Stumpy the old deputy saves the day and kills two of Burdette's gang at the jail.
13. c. Dude and Colorado sing Get Along Home Cindy.
14. c. Chance shoots dynamite at the entire gang and they all surrender.
15. d. Feathers puts on a sexy costume to sing in and Chance threatens to arrest her.

NUMBER FIFTEEN: THE HORSE SOLDIERS

1. b. Before the Civil War started John Marlowe was a railroad engineer.
2. b. Col. Marlowe's secret mission is to destroy the railhead at Newton's Station.
3. c. William Holden played the second male lead in the film as Maj. Kendall.
4. c. Marlowe and Kendall disagree on how Marlowe treats his troopers.
5. b. Marlowe's wife died in his arms after she had needless surgery.
6. b. Marlowe calls Kendall croaker.
7. c. He splits his troops, sending one third back.
8. b. She is a southern spy.
9. b. Kendall refers to Marlowe as the Section hand.
10. d. Marlowe plans to take his troops to Baton Rouge.
11. c. Greenbriar
12. b. The old sergeant was played by Hoot Gibson.
13. c. Frees an old sheriff from two rebel deserters.
14. b. Constance Towers.
15. c. In a bit of John Ford humor, Wayne orders his trooper to spank the young military school cadet.
16. c. He is shot in the lower leg.
17. b. He places her bandana around his neck.

NUMBER SIXTEEN: NORTH TO ALASKA

1. c. Sam goes to Seattle to escort George's French fiancee back to Alaska.
2. c. Stewart Granger played George Pratt.
3. c. Frankie Canon was played by Ernie Kovacs.
4. c. Frankie tried to sell Sam a phoney diamond ring which shatters when Sam hits it with a whiskey bottle.
5. c. Sam finds a French call girl in a place called the Hen House and asks her to come to Alaska with him.
6. b. Big Sam enters and wins a tree climbing contest at a lumberman's picnic.
7. c. Fabian, who played the role of little Billy Pratt, was a rock n' roll star of the 1950's.
8. b. George forgives Sam for bringing Michelle but quickly discovers that Sam is in love with her.
9. c. Character actor Mickey Shaughnessy
10. b. Sam shouts that he loves her.
11. c. George happens to have on him a diamond ring that he bought from Frankie.

NUMBER SEVENTEEN: THE COMANCHEROS

1. c. Big Jake is a Texas Ranger.
2. b. Paul Regret is wanted for murder in Louisiana.
3. c. After burying some ranchers slaughtered by Indians Regret hits Big Jake on the head with the shovel.
4. b. Big Jake goes undercover as a gun runner.
5. b. Lee Marvin is wonderful as the evil Tully Crow.
6. c. When he takes his hat off we notice that part of his scalp is missing.
7. d. Crow thinks that Jake and Regret are partners after losing to them at poker.
8. b. Big Jake handcuffs Regret to an iron anvil while visiting a ranch family.
9. a. Regret rides off to get the Rangers during an Indian attack.
10. b. Regret is made a Texas Ranger and becomes free of the murder charge in Louisiana.
11. c. Regret falls in love with the daughter of the Comanchero leader.
12. b. Big Jake and Regret are hung from a large pole to die.
13. c. The Duke's son Patrick Wayne played Tobe.
14. b. Regret's girlfriend Pilar helps them get out of camp where they are saved by the company of Texas Rangers.
15. c. Regret calls him "My Friend."

NUMBER EIGHTEEN: THE WINGS OF EAGLES

1. b. Spig Wead was in the Navy.
2. b. Spig was a Navy pilot in the film and in real life.
3. c. Spig got up at night to go to his child's bedroom and fell downstairs breaking his neck in the fall.
4. b. Spig actually learned to walk again.
5. b. Spig began writing screenplays.
6. a. John Dodge is the movie name for John Ford who directed the film and in real life was a friend of Frank Wead.
7. c. Frank Wead suffered a heart attack while aboard ship.
8. c. Frank Wead wrote the screen play for They Were Expendable directed by John Ford which starred John Wayne in 1945.
9. c. In this film the Duke appeared without his toupee in the later scenes as Spig ages before his death.
10. b. The character of Judhead Carson was important because this old friend forced Spig to learn to walk again.
11. a. Dancer Dan Dailey played the role of Jughead Carson.
12. c. He was a Lieutenant Commander.
13. b. He was called the Commodore.
14. c. Clark Gable
15. a. The Japs bombed Pearl Harbor.

NUMBER NINETEEN: REAP THE WILD WIND

1. b. Jack Stuart is a merchant ship captain.
2. c. Ray Milland played the romantic lead.
3. c. Wayne was directed by Cecil B. DeMille.
4. b. The movie action takes place off the Florida keys.
5. c. Jack Stuart's sweetheart was played by Paulette Goddard.
6. b. Stuart is knocked unconscious by one of his crew and his ship is driven onto a reef and sunk.
7. b. Stuart deliberately runs his ship, the best of the shipline, onto a reef.
8. b. Veteran actor Raymond Massey played the evil King Cutler.
9. c. Loxi's cousin drowns while hiding in the cargo hole of Jack Stuart's ship.
10. b. John Wayne redeems himself when he saves Ray Milland from the giant squid and drowns.

NUMBER TWENTY: THE LONG VOYAGE HOME

1. d. The movie was based on several short plays by Eugene O'Neill.
2. b. Thomas Mitchell from the Stagecoach cast starred as Driscoll.
3. c. Wayne had to learn to speak with an accent.
4. d. The Duke's nationality was Swedish.
5. b. The Duke was a merchant marine sailor during World War II.
6. b. The Duke is not injured in a bar fight but his drink is drugged.
7. c. Ward Bond as Yank had a memorable death scene.
8. b. Wayne as Ole carries his pet parrot in a cage.
9. b. The man from the bar is holding Ole's parrot behind his back and the parrot starts to talk.
10. b. Ole promised not to get drunk so he asks for a ginger beer which is drugged.

NUMBER TWENTY ONE: THE HIGH AND THE MIGHTY

1. c. This was the first of the airplane disaster films with an all-star cast.
2. b. Wayne played the role of the middle aged co-pilot.
3. c. Dan Roman was injured in an airplane crash.
4. b. Dan is known as "Whistling Dan Roman".
5. b. Dan forces the pilot not to ditch the plane in the ocean.
6. d. Phil Harris was the only actor not to star with Wayne in other films.
7. d. Jan Sterling had not appeared with The Duke before this film.
8. b. The role was originally set to go to Spencer Tracy who backed out at the last minute and Wayne took the part.
9. c. When the Duke walks away at the end he is whistling The High and the Mighty which he whistled throughout the film.

NUMBER TWENTY TWO: TALL IN THE SADDLE

1. b. Rocklin leaves the table and goes upstairs for his gun.
2. c. Rocklin won with two pairs Kings up.
3. c. Arly fires five shots at him.
4. b. Rocklin grabs her forcibly and kisses her.
5. b. Rocklin gives back the borrowed horse and takes his saddle up to his room.
6. c. Rocklin finds a deck of marked playing cards in Judge Garvey's desk.
7. b. Rocklin was Red Kardell's nephew.
8. a. In a change of pace role Ward Bond played the town villian Judge Garvey.
9. c. Gabby Hayes played the crusty old stage driver Dave.
10. b. The man who shot at Rocklin in the line cabin dropped his tobacco pouch.

NUMBER TWENTY THREE: FLYING TIGERS

1. c. Jim goes to Rangoon to recruit new pilots for his Flying Tigers squadron.
2. b. Brooke is the squadron's nurse.
3. b. Wayne has to tell his wing man and second in command that he is grounded because of his failing eyesight.
4. a. John Carroll played the role of Woody.
5. c. For every Jap plane shot down the men got $500.
6. b. Jim Gordan is from San Francisco.
7. a. Woody calls Jim "Pappy".
8. b. Anna Lee played Wayne's love interest.
9. b. The Duke's plane is number 70.
10. c. Jim and Brooke sit in the restaurant listening to That Old Feeling.
11. a. Flying Tigers was The Duke's first war film.

NUMBER TWENTY FOUR: BACK TO BATAAN

1. a. The Duke is in the U.S. Army in this film.
2. b. Wayne as Col. Joe Madden is ordered to form a guerilla force to continue fighting against the Japs.
3. c. Bonifacio is the son of a well known and respected Filipino leader and patriot.
4. b. A young Anthony Quinn starred as the Filipino soldier Andres Bonifacio.
5. a. He thinks his sweetheart has become a traitor and collaborator with the Japs.
6. c. A Jap soldier finds the Army colonel insignia on the boy that Wayne gave him.
7. b. Wayne uses an old Filipino trick and hides under water breathing through hollow reeds.
8. b. He asks for more Japanese.
9. b. The guerillas fly an American Flag while waiting in a boat.
10. c. The battle for Leyte is supported in this film.
11. b. The film shows actual Prisoners of War from the Phillipines.

NUMBER TWENTY FIVE: HONDO

1. b. Hondo's dog is named Sam.
2. b. Hondo is carrying his Winchester rifle and his saddle bags. He does not have his saddle with him.
3. c. Hondo is currently employed as a civilian scout for the cavalry.
4. b. Hondo paid an Indian to beat Sam as a puppy so that he would smell Indians.
5. c. Hondo notices that the ranch is run down.
6. b. Mr. Lowe thinks that Hondo stole one of his horses and hires a man to help him kill Hondo in an ambush.
7. c. After Hondo kills Mr. Lowe in self defense he takes the photo of the Lowe boy.
8. c. The Apaches drop hot coals on Hondo's hand to see if he will cry out.
9. d. The Apache that Hondo defeats in a knife fight kills Sam with a lance.
10. b. Hondo gives Lennie his Winchester rifle.
11. d. Hondo did not feed the goats, the Lowe boy did.
12. b. Hondo tells Angie that he is part-Indian.
13. c. Hondo curls up with his handgun in his hand.
14. b. Hondo tells Angie that the truth is the most important thing to him.
15. c. Rather than just fighting in a circle, he breaks the circle three times and keeps the wagons moving forward.

NUMBER TWENTY SIX: THE SONS OF KATIE ELDER

1. b. The Duke as John Elder was a well known gunfighter.
2. b. Dean Martin as Tom Elder was part conman who pretended to sell his eye for money.
3. c. John Elder watched the burial service from the top of a nearby hill.
4. b. Mr. Elder is killed during a card game.
5. a. Big John stops the bully Curley from sticking the blacksmith's head in a pail of water by hitting him in the face with an ax handle.
6. b. They are framed for killing the sheriff.
7. c. They shoot their way out of an ambush.
8. b. Matt Elder dies in the ambush.
9. a. Tom Elder had a knife on him which Big John threw out the window.
10. d. Big John shoots off a barrel of gunpowder.

NUMBER TWENTY SEVEN: DARK COMMAND

1. b. The Duke punches men in the mouth so his partner can charge them money to pull out their teeth.
2. c. Gabby Hayes played Doc Grunch the dentist.
3. c. Bob Seton is a cowboy from Texas.
4. b. Roy Rogers played the role of Duke's girlfriend's brother Fletch McCloud.
5. a. The Duke is up against the confederate raider William Cantrell.
6. c. Bob Seton's handicap is that he cannot read.
7. b. Bob decides to run and is elected the town sheriff.
8. c. Bob is forced to drive his wagon off a cliff into the water below.
9. b. Pidgeon's mother played by Marjorie Main hits his gun as he is about to shoot the Duke.
10. a. Fletch McCloud (Roy Rogers) helps Bob escape from the Rebel camp.

NUMBER TWENTY EIGHT: OPERATION PACIFIC

1. c. The Duke played a character called Duke Gifford who commanded a submarine.
2. b. The Duke's ship is called the U.S.S. Thunderfish.
3. d. The Duke has to take the submarine down while the captain is on deck.
4. b. Bob Perry the kid brother is after the Duke's ex-wife.
5. c. Patricia Neal played Mary Stuart, the Duke's ex-wife.
6. d. The Duke's ex-wife is now a Navy nurse.
7. b. The Duke and his crew are trying to develop firing pins that work in their torpedoes.
8. c. Bob Perry is shot down and The Duke rescues him.
9. a. Before Bob Perry leaves The Duke's sub, Wayne pats him on the top of his head.
10. c. Wayne and Pat Neal starred as lovers in In Harm's Way. Ms. Neal again played a Navy nurse.

NUMBER TWENTY NINE: THE FIGHTING SEABEES

1. c. Donovan ran a civilian construction company.
2. b. During a Jap air attack three of his men are shot and he takes his civilians out against the Jap forces.
3. c. When Wedge Donovan joins the Navy they give him the rank of Lieutenant Commander.
4. b. Susan Hayward had appeared with the Duke in Reap the Wild Wind in 1942.
5. a. The Duke who is usually light on his feet does the jitterbug and falls on the dance floor.
6. c. Donovan's oldest friend and mentor is killed by a Jap sniper.
7. b. Commander Yarrow tells him to hold and also that he is going to court martial him later.
8. c. The Duke uses a tractor to set an oil tank on fire to flood the valley and burn the Japs.
9. c. The Duke is killed by a Jap sniper but his plan works and the Japs are defeated.
10. b. The Duke tells Susan Hayward he cares for her while she is fighting for her life.

NUMBER THIRTY: THE ALAMO

1. c. The Duke played Col. Davy Crockett.
2. b. Davy only brought 23 men with him when he joined the Texans at the Alamo.
3. c. Davy wrote a fake letter from the Mexican General Santa Ana threatening his men if they fought with the Texans.
4. c. Davy gave Col. Travis a pack of cigars as a gift.
5. b. Davy surprises and impresses Col. Travis with his detailed knowledge of the political and military situation in Texas.
6. d. Everyone knows that Davy was stabbed with a lance then throws himself and his torch into the gunpowder.
7. a. Wayne originally intended to play the role of General Sam Houston.
8. b. Richard Boone had the small role of Sam Houston.
9. c. Frankie Avalon played the role of the messenger Smitty.
10. b. They steal the Mexican's herd of long horn cattle.
11. c. Congressman Crockett.
12. b. He is stabbed in the chest by a lance.

NUMBER THIRTY ONE: ANGEL AND THE BADMAN

1. b. Angel and the Badman was the first film that the Duke produced.
2. c. The Duke has a Winchester tied to his right leg when he falls from the horse.
3. b. Quirt Evans the Duke's character rode with Wyatt Earp.
4. b. The Quaker farmer puts the Duke's empty gun in his hand and he falls asleep.
5. c. The farmer and his pretty daughter are Quakers.
6. b. Marshal McClintock knows Quirt and states that he always wanted to hang him with a new rope.
7. a. McClintock gets Quirt's six shooter.
8. c. Quirt survives an ambush by driving his wagon off a cliff into a river then they hide under a nearby waterfall.
9. b. Quirt sends the town telegraph operator to tell the three gunman that he's waiting for them in the street.
10. b. Marshal McClintock shoots and kills the three gunman before they can draw on Quirt.

NUMBER THIRTY TWO: ROOSTER COGBURN

1. c. Rooster's first name is Ruben.
2. c. The court felt that he had killed too many criminals as a peace officer.
3. d. The gang ambushed and killed a cavalry patrol and stole their explosives.
4. b. This film was the first pairing of the Duke with legendary Katharine Hepburn.
5. c. Rooster respects Eula a little more when he sees that she is a crack shot with a rifle.
6. b. Many critics had compared and called this film the western African Queen.
7. b. Rooster was a peace officer in the state of Arkansas.
8. b. Rooster was a deputy Marshal for six years before his forced retirement.
9. b. Rooster had shot 64 suspects.
10. b. Miss Eula Goodnight was a proper lady from Boston.
11. b. Rooster called her "sister".
12. c. Rooster mutters that if they survive the rapids he will stop drinking.

NUMBER THIRTY THREE: McLINTOCK

1. c. George Washington McLintock
2. b. He hasn't lost his temper.
3. c. She wants to finalize their divorce.
4. b. He throws his hat atop the weather vane.
5. c. four years
6. b. He plays chess.
7. c. GW had not lost his temper in 40 years.
8. c. 310 times
9. c. He calls him Big McLintock.
10. c. He falls down three times.
11. b. They are Comanches.
12. c. He wants to give it to the government for a park.

NUMBER THIRTY FOUR: BIG JAKE

1. b. Big Jake comes home to learn that his grandson has been kidnapped. He starts out after the kidnappers.
2. c. For some unexplained reason they think Big Jake is dead.
3. b. Big Jake stops some cattlemen from hanging a sheep herder. The leader of the cattlemen was played by Jim Davis.
4. b. Michael Wayne was not in this film.
5. b. Michael McCandles traveled by motorcycle.
6. c. The large trunk was filled with cut-up newspaper rather than ransom money.
7. c. Richard Boone played the role of John Fain the leader of the kidnappers.
8. b. Boone also thought that Big Jake had died and told him so.
9. b. Big Jake takes his big black dog with him.
10. c. Christopher Mitchum played Michael.
11. a. Bruce Cabot played Sam Sharpnose the old Indian scout.

NUMBER THIRTY FIVE: THE GREEN BERETS

1. b. The Duke is a full colonel in the U.S. Army Special Forces Green Berets.
2. c. The Duke and his men go behind enemy lines to kidnap a Viet Cong general.
3. b. Janssen played a newspaper reporter who is opposed to America's presence in Viet Nam.
4. c. The Duke accepts the torture because they found a dead green beret's lighter on the traitor.
5. a. The Duke's helicopter is shot down but he survives the crash.
6. b. George Takei played the role of a Vietnamese army captain.
7. c. Jim Hutton played the role of Sgt. Peterson the scrounger.
8. b. The Duke is saved from a deadly Viet Cong booby trap.

NUMBER THIRTY SIX: IN HARM'S WAY

1. c. The Duke's ship is at sea and a Jap torpedo hits the ship and Wayne is thrown against a wall and breaks his arm.
2. b. The Duke was a career Navy man who would not leave the service.
3. c. His southern commander in chief refers to the Duke as his General Grant.
4. b. He dislikes the boy's attitude and said he would like to throw him to the fishes.
5. b. Com. Eddington played by Kirk Douglas had raped a young nurse so his act was more suicidal than heroic.
6. a. The Duke's girl Maggie Haynes was the daughter of an army officer.
7. b. The Duke defeats the Jap fleet but is wounded and has his leg amputated.
8. c. The future Archie Bunker Carroll O'Connor had a small role as a junior deck officer.
9. b. The Duke's nickname as Rockwell Torrey is "The Rock."
10. a. Capt. Torrey taught at the Naval Academy.

NUMBER THIRTY SEVEN: WAKE OF THE RED WITCH

1. b. The Duke first appears on screen tied to a raft floating in the ocean.
2. c. The natives try to burn him at the stake
3. b. The Duke takes his best ship and sinks it.
4. c. The Red Witch is loaded with millions in gold.
5. c. The Duke drowns in the hold of a sunken ship for the second time. The first was in Reap the Wild Wind.
6. b. The girl's father makes her marry another man of great wealth.
7. a. The Duke sails his ship into the harbor and jumps off before it blows up.
8. b. A rainstorm puts out the fire.
9. c. Gail Russell played the Duke's lady.
10. b. The Red Witch drops off a reef and the Duke drowns with the gold.

NUMBER THIRTY EIGHT: THE TRAIN ROBBERS

1. b. Texas
2. a. The Union Side
3. c. He stole gold from a train.
4. b. He wants to shrink her shirt.
5. c. They go into Mexico.
6. b. She nearly drowns.
7. c. Gold hidden in abandoned railroad engine.
8. b. The Pinkerton agent shoots at her.
9. c. Ricardo Montalban
10. b. Matt Lowe was never married.

NUMBER THIRTY NINE: THE WAR WAGON

1. b. two years
2. b. Lomax shot the Duke but he lived.
3. a. He offers him a $100,000 share in the gold.
4. b. Lomax is a safe cracker.
5. c. The Duke takes back his hand gun.
6. b. The nitro hidden in the tackhouse safe.
7. c. The Indian starts a fight.
8. c. They don't blow up the entrance to the gold mine.
9. b. The Indians take the gold hidden in the flour.
10. c. He takes the Duke's horse and rides off.

NUMBER FORTY: THE COWBOYS

1. c. They go for the gold strike.
2. b. He visits the local schoolhouse.
3. c. Jebediah is black.
4. a. The Duke beats him bloody in a fight.
5. c. The Duke is shot in the back and dies.
6. b. Bruce Dern
7. b. They can't find his actual grave site.
8. b. The Duke shouts "We're burning daylight."
9. a. One
10. c. Old Iron Pants
11. b. Two

NUMBER FORTY ONE: FLAME OF THE BARBARY COAST

1. a. The Duke sells his ranch and buys a saloon.
2. c. Montana
3. b. San Francisco
4. c. The Duke learns how to cheat at poker.
5. c. The Duke wins at poker and buys his own saloon.
6. b. The Silver Dollar
7. b. The 1906 San Francisco earthquake

NUMBER FORTY TWO: TROUBLE ALONG THE WAY

1. d. The Duke is an unemployed football coach.
2. b. The Duke has only his daughter.
3. c. The Duke tells her he is a tycoon.
4. b. Creating a winning football team
5. c. The Duke falls off his chair.
6. b. Sherry Jackson
7. c. baseball
8. b. The Duke caught her cheating.
9. a. Rochester
10. b. He gives them a percentage of the profits from each game.

NUMBER FORTY THREE: DONOVAN'S REEF

1. c. Their destroyer was sunk by the Japs.
2. b. The Duke owns a shipping business.
3. c. They have the same birthday.
4. c. Innisfree
5. b. They flash the light on the lighthouse.
6. a. She falls into the water.
7. b. She is from Boston.
8. c. Her father married a native Princess and has three mixed children.
9. b. Cesar Romero
10. b. Casablanca
11. b. Amelia wins the race.
12. b. PAX

NUMBER FORTY FOUR: FLYING LEATHERNECKS

1. b. The wildcats
2. a. He believes in close air support for ground troops.
3. b. Guadacanal
4. b. mud Marines
5. b. He orders his men to look at the body.
6. a. He is always wearing cowboy boots.
7. b. He is sorry he ordered a sick pilot to fly.
8. c. Navaho
9. b. He gives him a Jap sword.
10c. He crashes his plane into a Jap bomber.

NUMBER FORTY FIVE: ISLAND IN THE SKY

1. c. The Duke is a civilian pilot.
2. a. The Duke is flying for the Army.
3. b. The Duke has to crash land in Labrador.
4. c. He will shoot them in the leg.

Answers
To The Standard John Wayne

NUMBER ONE: ALLEGHENY UPRISING

1. b. Frontiersman
2. c. Pennsylvania
3. b. dishonest traders
4. c. Claire Trevor
5. b. George Sanders
6. a. Brian Donlevy

NUMBER TWO: THE FIGHTING KENTUCKIAN

1. c. Alabama
2. b. She is French.
3. c. The Duke fakes playing a violin.
4. d. The Duke pretends to be a surveyor.
5. b. Oliver Hardy played Willie Paine.
6. b. The Duke borrows Willie's top hat.
7. c. The exiles are from France.

NUMBER THREE: IN OLD CALIFORNIA

1. a. Boston
2. b. The Duke is a druggist.
3. b. The Duke bends silver dollars.
4. b. The news of the gold strike saves him.
5. c. He wants to cure them of the epidemic.

NUMBER FOUR: DAKOTA

1. b. The Duke is from Chicago.
2. a. He is an agent for the railroad.
3. b. He wants to buy farmland for the railroad.
4. c. Bond walked with a cane.
5. b. His wife buys a river boat.
6. c. Vera Ralston
7. b. Walter Brennan

NUMBER FIVE: THE SPOILERS

1. b. The picture is set in Alaska.
2. a. He is mining for gold.
3. b. They accuse him of murder.
4. c. Marlene Dietrich
5. b. Randolph Scott

NUMBER SIX: LADY FOR A NIGHT

1. b. The Duke played a river boat gambler.
2. c. Memphis
3. b. She is accused of murder.
4. c. Joan Blondell had the lead role.
5. b. She owned a gambling ship.

NUMBER SEVEN: THE LADY FROM LOUISIANA

1. b. The Duke is an attorney.
2. a. Ona Munson
3. b. New Orleans
4. c. arch enemy

NUMBER EIGHT: IN OLD OKLAHOMA

1. b. Army Veteran
2. b. The rights for government oil land.
3. c. President Teddy Roosevelt
4. b. The Duke was a sergeant in the Rough Riders.
5. b. The Duke's girlfriend is a writer.

6. b. The Duke's first job is as a body guard.
7. a. His enemy has brought the oil pipe line.
8. c. Gabby Hayes

NUMBER NINE: CHISUM

1. c. The Duke is an aging cattle baron.
2. b. Chisum's ranch is in New Mexico.
3. c. His foe is trying to buy up Lincoln county.
4. b. Pat Garrett and Billy the Kid

5. c. Sally is his niece.
6. b. White Buffalo is a Comanche.
7. c. Billy the Kid is reading the Bible.
8. b. He opens a bank and general store.

NUMBER TEN: CAHILL, U.S. MARSHAL

1. c. The Duke goes up against five men.
2. b. The Duke sings Streets of Laredo.
3. c. Texas
4. b. He is wounded in the left shoulder twice.
5. b. He wears a black wrist band.

6. c. His sons help rob the local bank.
7. b. The Duke falls off his horse.
8. c. The Duke walks after them then buys a mule.
9. b. to get the bank robbers out in the open
10. c. Denver Pyle

NUMBER ELEVEN: EL DORADO

1. b. The Duke is riding an Appaloosa.
2. b. The Duke is described as the tall guy about six feet four.
3. b. J P Harrah has the same loop on his Winchester rifle.
4. a. The Duke's horse backs up pass the armed ranch hands.

5. a. He is shot in the right side of his back.
6. c. The rancher's daughter shoots him.
7. b. Cochise
8. c. His right hand goes numb.
9. b. He feels he owes the rancher.
10. c. He cannot shoot a gun.

NUMBER TWELVE: THE UNDEFEATED

1. c. The Duke is an ex-Union army colonel.
2. b. The Duke wanted him to call him colonel.
3. b. The Duke meets his former Confederate foe.
4. c. Rock Hudson
5. b. The two groups join forces against the Mexicans.
6. a. & c. LA Rams stars Merlin Olsen and Roman Gabriel appeared in this film with Wayne.

NUMBER THIRTEEN: RIO LOBO

1. b. The Duke was guarding the payroll train.
2. b. The Duke gets hit in the head and captured.
3. a. The Duke asks the Confederate officer who robbed the train to help him find the traitor.
4. c. This movie is a rehash of El Dorado which was a remake of Rio Bravo.
5. b. George Plimpton
6. c. Howard Hawks

NUMBER FOURTEEN: BIG JIM McLAIN

1. c. The spirit of Daniel Webster is called upon.
2. b. Duke is an investigator for the House Un-American Activities Committee.
3. c. Big Jim was in the Marines.
4. b. Old 76 was The Duke's height in inches.
5. b. The movie and action was filmed in Hawaii.
6. a. Duke's partner died of an overdose of truth serum.
7. b. Duke is searching for ten agents.
8. a. Duke is stationed in Washington, D.C.

NUMBER FIFTEEN: MCQ

1. c. Duke played a police detective.
2. b. MCQ lives on a boat.
3. c. Green Hornet
4. b. Duke borrowed $5,000 from his ex-wife.
5. c. Duke beat up a local drug dealer.
6. a. Myra calls him a bear.
7. b. Duke was looking for two million in drugs.
8. c. The stolen drugs were hidden in the trunk.
9. b. MCQ borrows a rapid firing automatic rifle.
10. b. MCQ's captain was not involved in the drug theft.

NUMBER SIXTEEN: BRANNIGAN

1. c. Brannigan is a Chicago cop.
2. b. Duke plays a police Lieutenant.
3. b. Brannigan's first name is Jim.
4. d. The contract is worth $25,000.
5. b. Duke goes to London.
6. c. Duke drinks Whiskey and Beer.
7. b. He is slightly smaller then the Statue of Liberty.
8. b. Brannigan's son is a District Attorney.

NUMBER SEVENTEEN: A LADY TAKES A CHANCE

1. b. The Lady is from New York.
2. a. Jean Arthur played the lead.
3. c. Duke is thrown on top of her at the rodeo.
4. b. She steals his horse's blanket.
5. c. Duke is a rodeo cowboy.
6. a. Duke's horse is named Sammy.
7. c. Duke likes Irish whiskey.

NUMBER EIGHTEEN: WITHOUT RESERVATIONS

1. b. The film is a light comedy.
2. c. Rusty falls in love with a writer.
3. b. The actors are on their way to Hollywood.
4. d. Gary Cooper does not appear in this film.
5. b. Claudette Colbert
6. c. Don DeFore

NUMBER NINETEEN: THE SHEPHERD OF THE HILLS

1. b. Duke played an Ozark mountain-eer moonshiner.
2. c. He was illegitimate.
3. a. Duke's mother's name was Sarah.
4. b. He had to kill the man who fathered him.
5. a. Duke gives her a lace collar.
6. b. Duke is shot by his father.
7. c. It was Duke's first technicolor film.
8. b. Harry Carey, Sr. is called the shepherd.

NUMBER TWENTY: SEVEN SINNERS

1. c. Duke is the son of an Admiral.
2. a. Duke gives her an English penny.
3. b. She is wearing an admiral's coat.
4. c. Bijou is a cafe singer.
5. b. Bijou throws the coin into the ocean.

NUMBER TWENTY ONE: REUNION IN FRANCE

1. b. Duke is shot down in France.
2. c. He hid his I.D. tag in the heel of his shoe.
3. b. They pretend to be lovers on the way home.
4. c. Joan Crawford is the star of the film.
5. b. Duke is pretending to be an American student.
6. c. Duke calls her Mike.
7. b. Duke is disguised as a chauffeur.
8. c. His real destination is London.

NUMBER TWENTY TWO: A MAN BETRAYED

1. c. Duke is a small town attorney.
2. b. The father is the town's crooked politician.
3. c. Frances Dee
4. a. The Duke is investigating the suspicious death of his friend.

NUMBER TWENTY THREE: THREE FACES WEST

1. a. The Duke is a farmer in this film.
2. b. The Duke leads the entire town to Oregon.
3. b. The top soil is blowing away.
4. c. Her boy friend tells her he is a Nazi.

NUMBER TWENTY FOUR: PITTSBURGH

1. c. Wayne starts out in a coal mine.
2. b. Wayne makes and loses a fortune in the coal industry.
3. c. America's entry into World War II changes The Duke.
4. b. Wayne plays an unfaithful husband.
5. b. a boxing match
6. c. Shemp Howard played the tailor.
7. b. Duke actually loses the fight to Scott.

NUMBER TWENTY FIVE: TYCOON

1. b. Duke is working in South America.
2. b. The tunnel roof keeps falling down on the workers.
3. a. The Duke is forced to marry the girl.
4. b. He dynamites the tunnel entrance.
5. b. He asks The Duke to build the bridge across the river.
6. b. Laraine Day
7. c. The bridge survives a violent flash flood.

NUMBER TWENTY SIX: CIRCUS WORLD

1. c. Duke was her mother's secret lover.
2. b. Toni's mother was a high wire aerialist.
3. b. Duke's performers do not quit his show.
4. b. Duke practices jumping into the saddle of a moving horse.
5. a. The Duke's lady had joined a convent.
6. b. Rita Hayworth

NUMBER TWENTY SEVEN: HELLFIGHTERS

1. b. The Duke is an oil well fire fighter.
2. c. He is crushed by the blade of a tractor.
3. b. Malaya
4. a. The workers were Australians.
5. b. ten years
6. a. The Duke goes to Venezuela.
7. b. He has to put out five oil well fires.

NUMBER TWENTY EIGHT: THE SEA CHASE

1. c. The Duke is sailing under a German flag.
2. c. Wayne is trying to avoid the British naval forces.
3. b. The blond is a German spy.
4. b. It is suggested that The Duke gets into the lifeboat with Elsa and finds safety in Norway.
5. a. Lana Turner
6. b. The British Flag is tattooed on his back. James Arness played the German sailor.

NUMBER TWENTY NINE: LEGEND OF THE LOST

1. b. The Duke is living in Timbuktu.
2. c. He has moved into the local jail.
3. c. Duke is a desert guide in this film.
4. b. The Duke rides a mule.
5. b. She is the local prostitute.
6. c. The treasure is buried in a bat cave.
7. c. Duke's mule is named Janet.
8. c. A camel caravan comes along and saves them.
9. a. The Duke is stabbed in the back.

NUMBER THIRTY: HATARI

1. b. The Duke is chasing wild animals for zoos.
2. c. The girl is a photographer.
3. b. Henry Mancini wrote the music.
4. c. Elsa Martinelli
5. b. Duke rides the left front fender of the chase truck.
6. c. A Rhino
7. b. Red Buttons calls him "Bawana."
8. c. Three baby elephants
9. b. She asks him how he likes to kiss.

NUMBER THIRTY ONE: BLOOD ALLEY

1. b. Duke is captured by the Chinese Communists.
2. c. He escapes dressed as a Russian officer.
3. b. He talked to his imaginary lady called "Baby".
4. c. They want Duke to take them to Hong Kong.
5. b. The old ferry boat was built in Sacramento.
6. c. Robert Mitchum

NUMBER THIRTY TWO: JET PILOT

1. c. The film was not released until 1957.
2. b. Wayne pretends to defect to the Russians.
3. c. They give him drugs to erase his memory.
4. b. He steals his wife the Russian spy.
5. b. He falls in love with the Soviet agent.
6. b. Howard Hughes.
7. c. Janet Leigh played the Russian pilot.

ANSWERS
To The Cameo Roles

1. b. Duke played a Roman Centurion.
2. c. Duke witnessed the death of Jesus Christ.
3. c. Kirk Douglas had the lead in the film.
4. b. Duke played a general in Cast A Giant Shadow.
5. c. Israel is the country.
6. c. Duke helps Israel get U.N. recognition.
7. b. John Ford directed Duke in his sequence.
8. c. Duke played General William T. Sherman.
9. b. Harry Morgan played in the scene with Wayne.
10. c. Angie Dickinson played Duke's wife.
11. b. George Gobel had the lead in the film.
12. a. Duke broke his ankle.
13. c. The troops used a toy metal clicker.
14. b. Duke was a Lieut. Colonel in the Army.
15. b. Duke is pulled by his troops in a wooden cart.

THE CONQUEROR

1. c. Duke played the part of Genghis Khan.
2. d. Duke was from Mongolia.
3. c. Susan Hayward played a Tartar princess.
4. b. Howard Hughes produced the film.

5. a. Her father had poisoned the Duke's father.
6. a. Duke survives by hiding in a cave.
7. b. Duke is made to pull her wagon.
8. a. He is asked to kill his best friend played by Pedro Armendariz.

THE BARBARIAN AND THE GEISHA

1. b. He was the first American Diplomat sent to Japan.
2. b. Sam Jaffe played the role of Henry Heusken.

3. a. Duke stands in front of the cannon.
4. b. He burns the village down.
5. c. Wayne is beaten by the small man.
6. b. The President was Franklin Pierce.

NUMBER ONE: THE JOHN FORD CONNECTION

1. c. Duke and Jack Ford made 14 films together.
2. a. Ford directed the Duke in four westerns. They were Stagecoach, Three Godfathers, The Searchers and The Man Who Shot Liberty Valance.
3. b. The Duke starred in four cavalry films for John Ford. They were Fort Apache, She Wore A Yellow Ribbon, Rio Grande and The Horse Soldiers.
4. a. Duke starred in three military related films directed by John Ford. The films were The Long Voyage Home, They Were Expendable and The Wings of Eagles.

5. b. The Ford/Wayne films won three Oscars. One for Stagecoach, one for She Wore A Yellow Ribbon and one for The Quiet Man.
6. c. The Duke appeared in Hangman's House.
7. b. The last film that Ford directed the Duke in was Donovan's Reef in 1963.
8. c. Monument Valley
9. e. The Duke had the lead in The Searchers.
10. a. The Duke called him Pappy
11. c. Ford was an Admiral in the US Navy.

NUMBER TWO: THE EARLY MOVIE YEARS

1. b. The Big Trail
2. c. Breck Coleman
3. d. Duke Gifford was the character in Operation Pacific made in 1951.
4. a. The Duke appeared as "Singin" Sandy Saunders.
5. b. The Duke played a pilot.
6. c. The Sea Spoilers was made in 1936.
7. e. The Duke played a hockey player in Idol of the Crowds.
8. c. The Duke's group was called The Three Mesquiteers.
9. b. Duke took lessons in throwing a tomahawk.
10. b. Hangman's House was the silent film he appeared in.
11. c. Duke's first speaking part was in Salute. He played a Naval cadet.
12. d. He appeared with Marlene Dietrich later in his long career.
13. d. The Duke played opposite Louise Brooks.
14. c. The Man From Monterey. Duke also used a sword years later in The Conqueror.
15. b. The horse's name was Duke.
16. c. For the role in The Big Trail Duke Morrison became John Wayne. However, it did require a special screen and was a box office flop.

NUMBER THREE: THE DUKE'S FAMILY ON FILM

1. c. The four children appeared in The Quiet Man.
2. b. Michael was cast as a guard in The Conqueror.
3. c. Patrick and John Ethan Wayne appeared with their dad in Big Jake.
4. b. Patrick and Aissa Wayne had parts in The Alamo.
5. c. Duke's youngest child Marisa appeared in The Shootist.

NUMBER FOUR: THE DUKE MOVIE MISCELLANY

1. c. E.T. was watching The Quiet Man.
2. d. Hugh O'Brien was the last to be killed.
3. b. & f. Joe Namath and Bobby Rydall never appeared with The Duke in films.
4. b. George Plimpton produced a documentary about his experience as a bit player in Rio Lobo.
5. c. Boone was killed in Big Jake and The Shootist.
6. c. The Duke did not wear a coonskin cap in The Shepherd of the Hills.
7. d. The Duke never played a Canadian.
8. b. The Duke's movies appeared on screen for 48 years from 1928 to 1976.
9. c. Wayne never made a movie with Jane Russell.
10. b. & d. Wayne played Kirby York in Fort Apache and Rio Grande.
11. b. The Duke was clean shaven in The Undefeated.
12. b. Hondo was made in 3-D.
13. b. & d. The Duke was up a pole in North to Alaska and Circus World.
14. b. The Duke made ten war films.
15. c. The Duke first saw combat in Flying Tigers.
16. a. Wayne wore a hairpiece first in Sands of Iwo Jima.
17. b. The long running television hit was Gunsmoke.
18. c. Duke was just a sailor in The Long Voyage Home.
19. c. The Horse Soldiers is not part of the Cavalry Trilogy.
20. b. Duke first starred with O'Hara in Rio Grande.
21. c. The last Wayne-O'Hara movie was Big Jake in 1973.
22. c. Tall in the Saddle was not included.
23. c. Montgomery Cliff first appeared in Red River in 1948.
24. b. Duke played a German sea captain in The Sea Chase.
25. c. Duke played a Swede in The Long Voyage Home.
26. d. Duke played Genghis Khan in The Conqueror.
27. c. Trouble Along The Way was a romantic story about football.
28. d. The Wild Goose II was named after John Ford's yacht.
29. b. Lee Marvin lives through Donovan's Reef.
30. b. The Duke was killed in The Cowboys.
31. c. Duke never made a film with his friend Gary Cooper.
32. c. They all played Indians.
33. b. Duke made a wrong decision in Reap The Wild Wind.
34. c. Duke was Big Jake Cutter in The Comancheros.
35. b. The Long Grey Line starred Tyrone Power.
36. b. Walter Huston never made a film with Wayne.
37. c. Wayne's voice was heard in a Wagon Train episode.
38. a. The Duke appeared on the first Gunsmoke.
39. b. & d. George Takei and Jeffrey Hunter.
40. c. Ringo's first name was Henry.
41. c. We don't know if he lived or died in The Sea Chase.
42. b. The line was from Without Reservations.
43. c. The Duke rode a mule in Legend of the Lost.
44. b. Duke was dressed as a Roman in The Greatest Story Ever Told.

45. c. Duke appeared without his hairpiece in The Wings of Eagles.
46. c. The one line cameo role was in The Greatest Story Ever Told.
47. c. The Duke called Jimmy Stewart "Pilgrim" in The Man Who Shot Liberty Valance.
48. c. Singing Sandy Saunders also known as John Wayne.

49. b. Johnny Mack Brown never played with the Three Mesquiteers.
50. c. Wayne appeared as Duke Morrison in Words and Music.
51. a. & d. Duke spanked his ladies in McLintock and Donovan's Reef.
52. b. Gary Cooper was the original choice for The Big Trail.

NUMBER FIVE: THE DUKE IN LOVE

1. j. (Rooster Cogburn)
2. g. (The Cowboys)
3. d. (McLintock)
4. c. (Circus World)
5. f. (Big Jake)
6. b. (In Harm's Way)
7. a. (The Man Who Shot Liberty Valance)
8. e. (The Shootist)
9. h. (Donovan's Reef)
10. i. (North to Alaska)

NUMBER SIX: THE DUKE'S LEADING LADIES

A.

1. h. (Reunion in France)
2. f. (Reap the Wild Wind)
3. g. (Legend of the Lost)
4. e. (Circus World)
5. c. (The Sea Chase)
6. d. (Hatari)
7. j. (The Train Robbers)
8. a. (Donovan's Reef)
9. i. (Rio Bravo)
10. b. (Jet Pilot)

B.

1. b. (Trouble Along the Way)
   e. (They Were Expendable)
2. c. (Angel and the Badman)
   f. (Wake of the Red Witch)
3. g. (The Shootist)
   i. (Blood Alley)
4. h. (Dakota)
   j. (The Fighting Kentuckian)
5. a. (In Harm's Way)
   d. (Operation Pacific)

C.

1. c. (Susan Hayward)
2. a. (Claire Trevor)
3. b. (Marlene Dietrich)
4. e. (Vera Miles)
5. d. (Maureen O'Hara)

NUMBER SEVEN: THE INDESTRUCTIBLE DUKE

A.

1. e. (Drowned by a giant squid)
2. f. (Died of multiple gun wounds)
3. a. (Shot in the back by a rustler)
4. b. (Died of old age)
5. h. (Shot in the chest by a sniper)
6. d. (Shot through the heart by a sniper)
7. c. (Stabbed with a lance)
8. g. (Drowns as ship drops off ledge)

B.

1. d. (They Were Expendable)
2. h. (Fort Apache)
3. g. (The Long Voyage Home)
4. c. (Angel and the Badman)
5. f. (True Grit)
6. e. (The Comancheros)
7. b. (Hondo)
8. a. (Rio Bravo)
9. j. (Dark Command)
10. i. (The Green Berets)

C.

1. g. (The Longest Day)
2. e. (In Harm's Way)
3. b. (The Wings of Eagles)
4. f. (They Were Expendable)
5. c. (Red River)
6. d. (Big Jake)
7. a. (Hondo)

NUMBER EIGHT: THE DUKE GOES TO WAR

1. d. (Flying Tigers)
2. o. (Back to Bataan)
3. l. (They Were Expendable)
4. n. (Rio Grande)
5. j. (She Wore A Yellow Ribbon)
6. m. (Sands of Iwo Jima)
7. g. (Operation Pacific)
8. e. (Flying Leathernecks)
9. i. (The Wings of Eagles)
10. h. (The Horse Soldiers)
11. k. (The Longest Day)
12. f. (In Harm's Way)
13. a. (The Green Berets)
14. b. (Cast A Giant Shadow)
15. c. (The Fighting Seabees)

NUMBER NINE: THE DUKE IN UNIFORM

1. b. (In Harm's Way)
2. c. (Cast A Giant Shadow)
3. e. (The Longest Day)
4. f. (Sands of Iwo Jima)
5. d. (Fort Apache)
6. g. (Back to Baatan)
7. a. (Seven Sinners)
8. k. (The Wings of Eagles)
9. h. (Flying Leathernecks)
10. j. (Operation Pacific)

NUMBER TEN: THE DUKE OUT OF UNIFORM

1. i. (Trouble Along the Way)
2. f. (The Quiet Man)
3. e. (Pittsburgh)
4. l. (The High and the Mighty)
5. c. (The Shepherd of the Hills)
6. j. (In Old California)
7. h. (Tycoon)
8. g. (Legend of the Lost)
9. k. (Hellfighters)
10. m. (Brannigan)
11. d. (Lady for a Night)
12. b. (Lady From Louisiana)
13. a. (Three Faces West)
14. o. (Circus World)
15. n. (Hatari)
16. p. (The Spoilers)

NUMBER ELEVEN: THE DUKE ON LOCATION

1. c. (Tycoon)
2. d. (Hatari)
3. b. (Legend of the Lost)
4. a. (Circus World)
5. h. (The Barbarian and the Geisha)
6. g. (Island in the Sky)
7. f. (Big Jim McLain)
8. i. (Jet Pilot)
9. k. (Blood Alley)
10. e. (The Green Berets)
11. j. (Brannigan)
12. l. (They Were Expendable)

NUMBER TWELVE: IMAGES OF THE DUKE

1. j. (True Grit)
2. e. (Sands of Iwo Jima)
3. h. (The Quiet Man)
4. i. (She Wore A Yellow Ribbon)
5. a. (The Searchers)
6. k. (Stagecoach)
7. d. (The Man Who Shot Liberty Valance)
8. f. (The Shootist)
9. l. (Red River)
10. n. (Fort Apache)
11. m. (The Alamo)
12. t. (Hondo)
13. g. (McLintock)
14. r. (Reap the Wild Wind)
15. q. (Rio Bravo)
16. s. (Three Godfathers)
17. u. (The Fighting Seabees)
18. o. (The Horse Soldiers)
19. p. (Rio Grande)
20. c. (The Cowboys)
21. b. (The Sons of Katie Elder)

NUMBER THIRTEEN: THE DUKE'S SCREEN TALK

1. c. (The Searchers)
2. d. (The Sands of Iwo Jima)
3. b. (She Wore A Yellow Ribbon)
4. a. (The Quiet Man)
5. e. (The Man Who Shot Liberty Valance)
6. f. (True Grit)
7. h. (McLintock)
8. i. (Hondo)
9. j. (Rio Bravo)
10. g. (The Shootist)

Arons, Rana., ed. A TRIBUTE TO JOHN WAYNE. New York: Platinum Publications, Inc., 1979.

Bishop, George. JOHN WAYNE THE ACTOR/THE MAN. Thornwood: Caroline House Publishers, Inc., 1979.

Boswell, John and David, Jay. DUKE: THE JOHN WAYNE ALBUM. New York: Ballantine Books, 1979.

Cameron, Ian. ADVENTURE IN THE MOVIES. New York: Crescent Books, 1973.

Carpozi, George. THE JOHN WAYNE STORY. New York: Dell Publishing Co., Inc., 1974.

Cavinder, Fred, ed. A TRIBUTE TO JOHN WAYNE. The Saturday Evening Post, August 1979.

Fryd, Peter, ed. A TRIBUTE TO JOHN WAYNE: THE DUKE. New York: Bunch Books, 1979.

Goldstein, Norm. JOHN WAYNE: A TRIBUTE. New York: Holt, Rinehart and Winston, 1979.

Hanna, David. JOHN WAYNE. New York: Lorelei Publishing Co., 1979.

Little, Bessie, ed. JOHN WAYNE: DUKE'S OWN STORY. New York: Reliance Publications, Inc., 1979.

Martin, Bob and Woods, Bob. JOHN WAYNE & THE GREAT COWBOY HEROES. New York: O'Quinn Studios, Inc., 1979.

Perlmutter, Tom. WAR MOVIES. Secaucus: Castle Books, 1974.

Shaw, Sam. JOHN WAYNE IN THE CAMERA EYE. New York: Peebles Press International, Inc., 1979.

Stacy, Pat. DUKE: A LOVE STORY. New York: Pocket Books, 1983.